THE ANATOMY OF POETRY

THE
ANATOMY OF POETRY

by

MARJORIE BOULTON

M.A., B.Litt.

WITH A FOREWORD BY
L. A. G. STRONG

ROUTLEDGE & KEGAN PAUL LTD

Broadway House, 68–74 Carter Lane

London

First published in 1953
by Routledge & Kegan Paul Limited
Broadway House, 68–74 Carter Lane
London E.C.4
Printed in Great Britain by photolithography
Unwin Brothers Limited
Woking and London

Second impression 1955
Third impression 1959
Fourth impression 1962
Fifth impression 1968
Sixth impression 1970

ISBN 0 7100 1099 0 (c)
ISBN 0 7100 6091 2 (p)

To
HENRY TREECE
the best teacher I ever had
and a most loyal
and understanding friend

FOREWORD

A BOOK about poetry which can be used in the classroom needs first of all to be honest and sensible. This book is very honest and sensible. It is also practical, and written by someone who has never allowed classroom work to dull her original response to poetry.

I am by nature and from experience suspicious of classroom attempts to explain works of art, since they are so often the work of prosaic minds incapable of appreciating anything but rules. Such teachers can comment upon structure and metre, but are insensitive to rhythm, read badly, and never get beyond a strictly rational account of what they think the poem is about. They are of the kind that asks children to paraphrase a poem, and award marks for the result.

This little book is an excellent corrective to any such malpractice. The author shows that it is possible to approach a poem in a business-like manner without spoiling its magic or losing enjoyment of its music. She shows, in fact, that no other approach *is* business-like, since no other will get near the reality of the poem. I do not agree with everything she says, but I commend her book most warmly as a sincere and useful introduction to a great subject; clear-headed, realistic, and easy to understand.

L. A. G. STRONG

CONTENTS

AUTHOR'S INTRODUCTION

I HAVE tried to prevent this from becoming an ill-tempered book, but it was written as the result of prolonged irritation. As a student of literature and later as a teacher in school, emergency training college and three-year training college, as a private coach and lecturing for the W.E.A., I have steadily accumulated exasperation at being unable to find and recommend to my pupils a book on the technique and content of poetry which should be what I wanted them to read. The book I required must be fairly small; it must be more than a string of technical terms yet explain all the usual technical terms; it must have plenty of examples to avoid misunderstanding; it must draw its examples from a wide range of English poetry; it must be up to date, explaining such things as pararhyme and free verse; and, since most of my pupils are trying to take examinations, it must be helpful to the examination candidate without killing poetry by an excess of formalism and pedantry. Never having found such a book, and finding that the appendix on poetry at the back of the grammar book is often too dry to be swallowed, the mass of excellent advanced criticism available to-day rather too rich to be digested by the inexperienced, I have tried to write the book myself and to give an outline of the subject which shall begin at the beginning, but be sufficiently comprehensive on its elementary level. I hope it may be useful to students and teachers.

I should have liked to use more contemporary poetry, but have been deterred by the obstacles of copyright; however, I have tried to encourage the student to read contemporary work. I have made no attempt at giving a potted history of literature such as is readily available elsewhere. This is frankly a technical book, but I have tried to bear in mind that the only sound reason for examining poetry technically is that this adds to our enjoyment.

I have to acknowledge the kindness of Faber & Faber Ltd. for permission to quote from W. H. Auden's 'As he is' (in *Collected Shorter Poems*, 1950), and from Louis MacNeice's 'Aubade' (in *Poems*, 1935); of Mr. George Fraser for permission to quote from one of his sonnets; of Routledge & Kegan Paul for permission to use a quotation from Sidney Keyes' 'The Wilderness' (in *The Cruel Solstice*, 1944); of Chatto & Windus for permission to quote three extracts from poems by Wilfred Owen from *The Poems of Wilfred Owen*, 1931; and of Mr. Robert Penn Warren for permission to quote from his poem *Original Sin*.

The help I have received in writing this book has really extended over at least the last fifteen years, for all kinds of educational experiences and chance remarks have contributed to it. However, I should like to mention particularly my friends and sometime colleagues, Miss Helen Smith, Miss Freda Sachse, Miss Grace Keenleyside, and Miss Mary Fowler, with all of whom I have had many stimulating discussions on poetry as well as many less bookish pleasures; my pupils of all ages from eleven to forty-five who have asked me difficult questions and sometimes helped me to knowledge by their alert suggestions, sometimes forced me to clarity by their misunderstandings; my mother, Mrs. E. M. Boulton, whose fresh and sincere approach to the arts is an inspiration to me; Mr. J. F. Danby, who has given me much mental stimulation and personal encouragement; Allan Jacobs, who read the first draft of this textbook and improved it by a number of pene-trating criticisms and thoughtful suggestions. A debt I can never hope to pay is acknowledged in my dedication.

I do not expect that everyone who reads this book will be satisfied; I shall never myself be satisfied with anything I write; but I hope that everyone who reads this book will learn something or be provoked to think.

Stoke-on-Trent
January 1953

I. THE IMPORTANCE OF FORM

Form: 1. Relative grouping of the parts of a thing.
WYLD: *Universal Dictionary of the English Language*

THE things that are most interesting and most worth having are impossible to define. If we use our common sense, and are careful to say enough, so as to exclude all other objects, we can easily explain what a shovel is, or a telephone, or a bracelet, or even something a little more symbolic such as a sceptre or a pound note. The fact that a man or woman deeply in love can 'find no words' is well known, though the attempt to find words has produced some of our greatest poetry; the fact that the mystic cannot describe intuitive experience accounts in part for the constant arguments on the subject of religion; and hundreds of serious thinkers have been defeated in the attempt to define beauty. Thus, in any analysis which aims at 'explaining' the beauty of poetry, we are to some extent trying to explain the inexplicable.

It does seem, however, that most people agree that one ingredient of beauty is form. Form implies some kind of definiteness or coherence, shape of some kind. A three-tier wedding cake has form, though not usually much beauty; a jelly which has been successfully turned out of a mould has form, though it would be more difficult to describe the exact shape of a moulded jelly than the wedding cake with its three cylinders

1

of different sizes. A cake which has crumbled or been cut into small pieces, a jelly which has failed to set and fallen into an amorphous mass on the dish, lacks form, and although this may be just as digestible and delicious as the geometrical cake or moulded jelly, it is much less attractive to the eye. We appreciate form in such matters as the arrangement of a room or a person's clothes, and dislike an untidy desk or a slovenly person; if we are at all conscious of the artistic possibilities of words, we do not like to hear a speech in which there is no logical sequence or to read a badly written article. Before I began to write this book, I made a plan so that it should at least have form and sequence.

There seems to be one interesting exception to this liking for form; I cannot explain it and shall content myself with stating it. It is that experience in which energy or magnitude alone gives us the feeling that 'this is beautiful'. I love thunder-storms and bathing in a rough sea; almost everyone is fascin-ated by a moving stream or river, or the sea, although water is one of the most formless things in the world; fire, snow and high winds give the same kind of excitement. While we wish to be generally in a state of balance and dignified tranquillity, those of us who are vigorously alive know that there are cer-tain states of overwhelming passion, indescribable tenderness or sudden elation that provide the most perfect and memor-able experiences of our lives. There seem to be two kinds of beauty to which we respond; the beauty of form and the beauty of splendid formlessness. Perhaps the second kind is either much more primitive, or much more advanced, than the first kind. However, the pleasure we find in poetry is usually dependent more or less on formal beauty; Whitman and some of Blake are the only obvious exceptions to this. We can assume that those experiences of beauty which can be analysed in an 'Anatomy of Poetry' are experiences of the beauty of form; the purpose of this book is to analyse the things that can be analysed, and a residue that is wonderful and cannot be explained will always be left.

Here I must give a warning. The analysis should not be studied too soon. Many people, trying to pass examinations or to please a teacher, have to approach poetry from the wrong end. This generally creates a distaste instead of increasing pleasure, and I should hate to think that this book would be used to give anyone a distaste for poetry.

If you do not care for poetry at all, please do not read any further. You cannot find anything to enable you to like poetry in any book except a book of . . . poems. If you feel you may be missing something by not liking poetry, go and buy or borrow some of the anthologies listed at the end of this book. Dip into them till you feel like reading something steadily; if you find a poem you like, try to read more poems by the poet whose name is at the bottom and so try gradually to expand your own capacity for poetry. Perhaps later you will be seized by a curiosity as to how these exciting effects are achieved; that will be the time to read this book and other books on the subject. Of course, if you are taking an examination in English Literature in six months, you had better not leave your textbooks alone till you can approach them in the right spirit; but so long as you know you are, from pressure of circumstances, approaching them in the wrong spirit, you will do yourself no harm.

Or perhaps you like to read poetry for yourself, but cannot bear to read it aloud or hear it read or recited. You may have heard it mangled and desecrated by little girls with coy squeaks, resentful little boys with raucous shouts or the wrong kind of teacher with soulful mooings. No wonder you feel that poetry brings out the worst in people! Try to listen to some of the readings on the wireless, or some really good records of spoken poetry by such speakers as Anthony Quayle, Mary O'Farrell, Cecil Day Lewis, Carleton Hobbs, T. S. Eliot, Edith Evans and John Gielgud; you will probably have one of the surprises of your life![1]

Ideally, literary criticism ought to arise out of pleasure. What should happen is that we find something delightful and for a time are satisfied with the delight; later, because the healthy mind seldom remains unmoving, we begin to wonder what is the cause of our delight. We may find, rather disconcertingly, that the cause has nothing to do with beauty. You may admire Donne's *Holy Sonnets* because you find them theologically sound, 'edifying'; if so, you may still be unable to see why they are better poetry than *Dare to be a Daniel*. You may like Harold Monro's *Milk for the Cat* because you enjoy the words in their aptness or because you like cats; in the latter situation, a live cat would give you more pleasure. If, however, you read and re-read a poem with pleasure and come ot notice that it has an agreeable rhythm, that the sequence of thoughts leads to a climax, that the rhymes are arranged in a pattern which provides reassuring repetitions and stimulating shocks, that the words are more appropriate than any you could put in their place . . . then you are practising the criticism of poetry.

In the early stages of discovering poetry for ourselves, we often find that to pull it to pieces in any way, even to repeat it

[1] A useful list of recorded poetry is issued by the Speech Fellowship. 1 Park Crescent, Portland Place, London W.1, for the price of 1s. 1d, post free. Anyone who is sick of the low standards prevalent in the speaking of poetry and speech in general might be cheered by joining this organization.

to another person, spoils it. Our first worthwhile experience of poetry is very personal, and we feel we want to keep it to ourselves much as we are inclined to be secretive about the beginnings of love in ourselves or about our experience of religion. We may feel that it is almost a profanation to investigate a poem too closely, just as it would be a liberty to be familiar with some person greatly respected. Yet once we have learned to pull poems to pieces intelligently, we find that our pleasure is made deeper by our understanding and the poem is not spoilt. A good poem is more interesting at the twentieth reading than at the first; we can always find something new in it; and, no matter how much we pull it to pieces, as soon as we stand back and look at it the pieces leap together once more.

Readers are often discouraged by the fact that a piece of criticism seems to contain a great many difficult words. Some of them are words which are a stumbling-block to poor spellers; *onomatopoeia* and *alliteration* are among these. There is a reason for the use of these long words. It would be possible to dissect a rabbit and explain our dissection to someone else without using a single recognized anatomical expression; we could make up comprehensible names for ourselves, such as *breath-bags*, *food-bag*, *blood-tubes* and *think-stuff*; yet these terms, being unfamiliar, sound uncouth and childish, and we would actually prefer to use the words that are accepted already. Similarly, a set of defined terms to describe the technique of poetry saves time and misunderstanding. Sometimes it saves too much time, as when a student uses a critical term without knowing the exact meaning, in the hope that it may give the right impression. These terms should be methods of communication and not methods of impressing people with our knowledge. It is as well to learn the critical terms, and a good many will be explained in the course of this book; but what are you to do if you see something in a poem on which you would like to comment, but for which you do not know a special name? Why, simply comment on it in your own words! The proper term would merely make things a little shorter; if you are intelligent enough to be enjoying poetry, you know enough about words to be able to put together some expression for yourself.

We always find something in a poem that we cannot analyse because it exists only in the poem as a whole. If we are trying to understand why a poem delights us, we separate the different parts; the reason for this is the crudely practical one that, though we can perceive several things at once, we cannot describe the several things that we perceive at once, all at the same time; we cannot think two complete sentences simultaneously. When we have separated the various things that go to make a poem what it is, we shall find that one thing is missing; part of the beauty of a poem, part of its form, is the way in which all the component parts are appropriate to each other and fit together. Obviously we cannot analyse this, any more than, when we dissect a rabbit, we can produce its life as a component part. A poem, unlike a rabbit, can be brought to life again after being dissected, but the vital unity can never be adequately defined.

We can usefully distinguish and discuss a number of aspects of form in poetry. The form of poetry is often more obvious than the form of prose, partly because poetry, though the most beautiful form of literature, is also historically the most primitive. The earliest poetry was, so far as we know, social in purpose: the incantation, the rite, the carol, the record of the tribe, the ballad; they were associated with ritual, dance or feasting. Nowadays poetry tends to be a personal, intimate, even introspective activity, though the growing popularity of the art of Choral Speaking suggests that there is still room in a self-conscious and sceptical society for a social and ritual function of poetry. Poetry, because of its primitive element, has perhaps more physical form than any other kind of literature. By *physical* I do not of course mean *material*; the *Encyclopaedia Britannica* is a more impressive mass of paper and binding than the *Sonnets* of Shakespeare; I mean that much of the form of poetry can be perceived physically, by the ear and eye, without any intellectual process occurring. Very small children enjoy things that have a marked rhythm, and most of us have had the experience of being captivated by the sound of a poem without fully understanding the words.

In criticism, as often in life, everything is connected with everything else, but to simplify this book I am going to separate the Physical Form and the Mental Form of poetry. The Physical Form is the appearance on paper, and, much more important, the sound of poetry. It may be either the sound when poetry is read to us, or the sound we hear mentally when we read it to ourselves. It includes: rhythm, rhyme, intonation and various kinds of echo and repetition. Mental Form might be described as Content in the usual sense of the word when applied to literature; it includes: grammatical structure; logical sequence; the pattern of associations; the use of a dominant image; the pattern of image and emotion. All these things combine to give a good poem its power over our imagination.

II. THE PHYSICAL FORM
OF POETRY

Untwisting all the chains that ty
The hidden soul of harmony.
MILTON: *L'Allegro*

IT is never possible to distinguish physical form completely from mental form, for the two are inter-related.
We do not, indeed, know the exact relationship of our
physical to our mental being, the extent to which our bodily
condition causes our temperament or the exact process by
which the mass of stuff known as a brain makes the intangible
things called thoughts. Indeed, the mystery of the relationship
of physical and mental is one of the mysteries that provides
material for much art and speculation. Whenever I am trying
to explain something quite clearly, I am hindered by an embarrassing awareness that everything is mixed up with everything else. I cannot hope to unmix them completely; I can
only try, by means of a few deliberate over-simplifications, to
make the study of poetry more comprehensible to the inexperienced reader. When I write about physical and mental
form, I am not forgetting that as soon as we begin to define
the physical form of a poem, we have not merely had a physical experience of it, but have thought about it; when I speak
of the mental form of a poem, I do not dispute that we hear or
read something by means of our ears or eyes, and that this is a

8

physical experience. I hope the reader will also remember these facts, so that he or she is not carrying on a continuous argument with me all through this book!

It is always misleading to separate the physical and mental form of a poem so far as to allow ourselves to say: 'What does it mean?' The poem means *itself*; if it could be given to us in a prose paraphrase without losing all its beauty, there would have been no point in writing it as a poem. The poem is a combination of physical and mental form and we ought to remember all the time that when we separate these in order to define or discuss them we are no longer discussing the poem. An analogy may be drawn from human personality. What am I? The answer to this question depends on what aspect of the whole that is *I* is under discussion. I am, among other things: a woman; a British subject by birth; the author of this book; five foot five; a training college lecturer; a native of the Potteries; a dear daughter; a nuisance. I am all these in different functions and many more things besides, but none of these are Me. To come up to me in the street and say 'What are you?' or 'What do you mean?' would be ridiculous. I am a complicated personality, with a physical existence and a mental existence, both governed by very complex interrelated laws. Similarly, it is ridiculous to ask what a poem *is* or *means* unless we specify what we, at the moment, want to know about it. It is reasonable to ask what Milton means by:

> Ring out, ye crystal spheres!

if we do not know enough about early astronomy to understand the allusion to the 'crystalline sphere' that was once thought to exist above the visible sky. This is a sensible question that has an answer. But if we take the whole beautiful verse and ask what it means:

9

> Ring out, ye crystal spheres!
> Once bless our human ears,
> If ye have power to touch our senses so;
> And let your silver chime
> Move in melodious time;
> And let the base of heaven's deep organ blow;
> And with your ninefold harmony
> Make up full consort to the angelic symphony.

the only proper answer is to repeat the verse again. Later in this book I shall give a few rough prose paraphrases of poems; but they are not, as the reader will see, substitutes for the poems, merely rather dull commentaries to illustrate some point I wish to make. Milton's *Ode on the Morning of Christ's Nativity* is a wonderful poem; we must not ask what it means, but what it feels like when we hear it; it is a fusion of imagination, speculation, learning and masterly verse techniques into one whole which is a work of art.

The most dangerous enemies of poetry in general or of particular groups of poets are those usually well-meaning people who go about saying: 'What does it mean?' Such people are trying to divorce the mental form, or rather a small part only of the mental form (the factual content in its logical sequence) from the totality of the poem, the unique whole that is made up of many mental and physical ingredients. You cannot take an egg out of a cake that has been baked!

When, throughout this textbook, I make distinctions of the various ingredients of poetry, I do so only because it is impossible to talk about two things at once. If I could explain how the various things were fused together to make the whole poem, I should not be a writer of textbooks, but a critical genius.

A rough distinction between sound and sense is perfectly reasonable. There is a real difference between, say, 'The cat sat on the mat' and 'The feline domestic pet was in a seated posture on the small portion of thick fabric'. The stupidest person is conscious of a difference; since the meaning of both statements is the same, the difference must be in the sound. Of this we can say that the first version is shorter and monosyllabic and that, as vowel and consonant are heard three times in the same relationship, it has a kind of crude pattern. This is a (very dull) critical statement about physical form only. Thus we can have two statements with exactly the same meaning but greatly differing in physical form; it would, however, be impossible to have two statements with exactly the same physical form and different meanings, for the fact that certain groups of sounds are assumed to have fixed meanings (or a group of possible meanings) is the basis of language.

Can it be argued that 'You are a beauty!' said in a tone of rapt admiration as by a lover to his lass, and 'You *are* a beauty!' said in an ironical tone by a gardener to a friend who has just plumped a careless foot into a row of seedlings, are two statements with the same physical form but different meanings? No, for the difference in meaning is shown by the intonation, which is immediately perceived by the ear. Everyone who has been to school has at some time heard a poem spoilt by stumbling, mumbling, stupid, or monotonous reading; that a poem can be spoilt by a bad vocal interpretation shows that the intonation is part of the physical form the poet intended. We often find that an argument about the vocal interpretation of a poem may go very deeply into the meaning of a poem.

For a poem to have significant physical form to the eye is not unknown, though it has never been common in English poetry. (I say *significant*, since everything that is seen, even a beetroot stain on the table-cloth, has *some* form to the eye.) Puttenham, in his *Arte of English Poesie*, 1589—one of the early books in English on the technique of poetry—gives examples of 'shaped poems'. These suggest Puzzle Corner in the newspaper rather than the outpourings of genius, but no doubt provided much harmless and elegant intellectual exercise. In the seventeenth century, George Herbert and Robert Herrick, poets with a fine lyrical gift, also wrote poems which could be fitted into pictorial shapes on the printed page:

The Pillar of Fame

Fame's pillar here, at last, we set,
Outduring marble, brass or jet,
Charm'd and enchanted so
As to withstand the blow
Of overthrow;
Nor shall the seas
Or outrages
Of storms oe'rbear
What we uprear.
Tho' kingdoms fall,
This pillar never shall
Decline or waste at all;
But stand for ever by his own
Firm and well-fixed foundation.

HERRICK

Even to-day Dylan Thomas has a long and beautiful poem called *Vision and Prayer*, which is shaped on the page into six diamonds and six hourglasses, but also has sound-patterns of great beauty and intricacy. In the 1949 edition the diamonds have turned into triangles and the hourglasses into wings, so evidently the visible shape is decorative rather than an important part of the poem. Interesting though the 'shaped poem' is as a freak, it is not important in the study of poetry. One reason for this is that words of the same length in sound may be of different lengths when printed; a 'shaped poem' is usually a problem for the printer, as some special spacing is necessary to keep the shape; thus the whole technique is rather unreal.

We do, of course, notice the form of a poem on a page when we begin to read. There is a real difference, even visually, between:

> For a day and a night Love sang to us, played with us,
> Folded us round from the dark and the light;
> And our hearts were fulfilled of the music he made with
>   us,
> Made with our hearts and our lips while he stayed with
>   us,
> Stayed in mid-passage his pinions from flight
> For a day and a night.
>
> SWINBURNE: At Parting

and

> With serving still
> This have I won,
> For my goodwill
> To be undone.
>
> And for redress
> Of all my pain
> Disdainfulness
> I have again.

> And for reward
> Of all my smart
> Lo, thus unheard
> I must depart!
> WYATT: *His Reward*

As soon as we see these two poems on the page we know that the vocal interpretation will be quite different. Indeed, I think it is safe to say that if they were printed somewhat differently:

> For a day and a night
> Love sang to us,
> Played with us,
> Folded us round
> From the dark and the light;
> And our hearts were fulfilled
> Of the music he made with us. . . .
>
> With serving still, this have I won,
> For my goodwill to be undone,
> And for redress of all my pain,
> Disdainfulness to have again. . . .

we should read them aloud somewhat differently, especially the Swinburne; the position of the line-endings is an indication to the reader of the correct vocal interpretation.

Dismissing visual form, however, as relatively unimportant —and, indeed, many of us have our first experience of violent delight in poetry from hearing it read aloud—we find that the physical form of poetry is mainly a pattern of sounds. At the risk, once again, of making false statements by over-simplification or excessive subdivision, we can divide the pattern of sound into two important categories, adding two less important categories. First and most obviously important is rhythm. Rhythm will need two long chapters to itself; it is often misunderstood; in the course of an enthusiastic study of poetry I have been forced to realize that everything I was taught at school about metre, before the sixth form, was wildly misleading, though my teachers were conscientious. This reluctant conclusion is the chief driving force behind this book, for of all the misconceptions about poetry that are current, what I like to call 'ke-bonk, ke-bonk', is the most disastrous.

Secondly, there is what I shall allow myself, for want of a better term, to call 'phonetic form'; I refer to patterns made up of resemblances, repetitions or sharp differences of vowel and consonant sounds placed in relation to one another. There is no merit in learning a list of critical terms, yet I am now going to burden the reader with a number of terms not, so far as I know, used before; they are a little uncouth, but I wish to leave the customary terms alone until there is no longer the risk of their being used glibly as a disguise for lack of knowledge or interest. To use new terms at least forces the reader to grasp the definitions.

Less important, there may also be a pattern of intonation, which, though part of the mental form, is part too of the physical form; there may be repetition of a kind which is more a part of the physical than of the mental form. Both kinds exist, as well as a combination of both. A study of the different uses of repetition will provide our bridge between physical and mental form.

Here I will release one of the many bees of Helicon that inhabit my bonnet. I am convinced that much of the rather anxious confusion about poetry that is to be seen in both young students and older readers is caused by an education that has depended too much on silent reading and has cultivated silence as a virtue, too little on any human voice except the didactic voice of the professional teacher; unfortunately, trained voices are rare, and untrained voices, especially in the teaching profession, are liable to lose their natural beauty and freshness through strain. Poetry, as much as drama, is meant to be performed, to be heard rather than read with the eye. When working in an emergency training college I found that a large number of students of all ages, who, if anything, rather disliked poetry after the dull experiences of their schooldays, rapidly developed interest, liking and an intelligent approach after hearing poetry read to them by me, with a voice not then trained and very far from beautiful, but with at least some regard for the sound and the meaning. We can read poetry silently and lose ourselves in a pleasant, vague mist of words; but to try to read it aloud properly forces us to pay full attention to it. As compared with Written English, Spoken English as a subject in schools is in its infancy, and a general raising of the standard of speech in our schools would probably do more for poetry even than a large subsidy to publishers.

III. RHYTHM

(A) METRE

'What needs this iterance, woman?'
SHAKESPEARE: *Othello*

WE must begin by making a distinction between rhythm and metre; unfortunately textbooks and teachers do not all agree on the correct use of these terms, and the student should always be careful to find out the exact sense in which these words are being used.[1] Both words, when used concerning English poetry, refer to the pattern of stresses. Rhythm I shall take as meaning every possible aspect of this, metre as meaning the symmetrical, repetitive pattern of stresses. Rhythm thus includes metre but metre is a relatively small part of rhythm. At school we generally learn about metre only—to 'scan' verses—and this is so dull that we seldom go further to enjoy the real beauties of rhythm. To see a class studying a poem and working out the metre with a loud *ke-bonk*, *ke-bonk* of a pencil on the desk is a most depressing sight. If poetry really moves in this wooden-legged swing, it is not surprising that many sensible people do not like it; ordinary speech is so much more varied, subtle and interesting!

[1] The student should also be careful to SPELL *rhythm* correctly; it is something of a favourite mistake.

17

English verse rhythm depends upon the arrangement of stresses. There are a number of ways of marking stresses when we are analysing the rhythm of a poem. Some books use the breve (ᴜ) and macron (–), but these are not really suitable for English, as they denote long and short syllables; more will be said about this presently. Some books and teachers use a small cross (x) for an unstressed syllable, and a stroke (/) for a stressed syllable. I was once taught to use an x for an unstressed syllable and an 'a' for a stressed syllable; the disadvantage of this is that it is customary to use letters of the alphabet in describing the pattern of rhymes, and to use letters for both metre and rhyme, e.g. 5xa,ababcc, is rather confusing. As we can assume that if a syllable has not a strong stress it must be a weak stress, it seems reasonable to use a stroke (/) over each stressed syllable, a method used by several good authorities. This has the advantage of not cluttering the page with more symbols than are strictly necessary, and avoids the ugliness of making poetry look like algebra. Thus:

$$\overset{/}{\text{The}} \overset{/}{\text{cat}} \text{ sat on the } \overset{/}{\text{mat}} \text{ and } \overset{/}{\text{ate}} \text{ a } \overset{/}{\text{rat.}}$$

clearly indicates which are the stressed syllables. They are simply the ones to which we give more emphasis in natural speech. There are often occasions when I should like a more complicated notation allowing me to indicate both strong and medium stresses as well as unstressed syllables; for instance, in the above sentence the strongest stresses are *cat* and *rat* with *sat, mat* and *ate* as medium-strong or secondary stresses. This, however, would be too detailed for this book, and anyone who can hear at all can hear that some words in a sentence are more important than others.

In English there are two kinds of stress, which are comple-

mentary to one another. There is, first, the stress of emphasis.
There is a difference between:

> I want a básket of eggs (not a box)

and

> I want a basket of éggs (not of oranges).

In two different sentences the same word may be stressed or
unstressed, according to its importance:

I shall not vóte for Mr. Fáthead, but for Mr. Bríght.

I shall not vóte for Mr. Bright, but I will hélp him.

The first person is preferring one candidate to another; the
second person is presumably under twenty-one. Even a
usually unimportant word, such as a conjunction or preposi-
tion, may on rare occasions carry a strong stress:

> I said, go únder the bridge, not óver it.

> Are we allowed a fish course ánd a meat course here?

Common sense enables us to place the natural stress of speech
in sentences, whether in poetry or in prose; it should be
realized that any stressing of poetry which is contrary to the
stressing of normal speech is incorrect. We have to pay attention to the meaning when stressing a sentence, for otherwise
we may pass on our misunderstanding to everyone who
hears us.

So much for emphatic stress; in words of more than one
syllable there is usually one syllable stressed more than the
others. English is a very irregular language in this respect, so
much so, even, that a word like *contrast* may be stressed differ-

ently according to whether it is a noun or a verb, and many words change the position of the stress when a suffix is added. Foreigners often speak 'broken English' by misplacing the stresses, long after they have mastered our difficult grammar and idiom; even educated and intelligent people often stress a word wrongly the first time they meet it. The only certain preventative of such embarrassment is to look the word up in a dictionary before attempting to say it.[1] We habitually say:

carpet, kitten, accident, immaterial, retribution

and anyone who said:

carpet, kitten, accident, immaterial, retribution,

would immediately be recognized as a foreigner or ignorant. Any interpretation of the rhythm of a poem which forces such a distortion upon a word must be wrong.

The first cultural education given in this country was a classical education in which Latin and Greek were treated as if they were more important than the native tongue. There is much to be said in favour of classical learning, but the extension of its terminology into the study of English literature has done as much harm as good. Languages differ very much in structure; Latin and Greek are highly inflected languages, that is, languages in which the changing endings of words denote their exact grammatical function. English is very little inflected, and depends mainly upon a traditionally correct order of words. Unfortunately, since the study of Grammar in

[1] Any good English dictionary gives some indication of how a word should be pronounced, including the stress. The best dictionary for pronunciation only is Daniel Jones: *An English Pronouncing Dictionary* (Dent, 10s. 6d.).

England was originally the study of Latin and Greek grammar, the formal grammar of English is overloaded with Latin terms that do not really suit our language, and, on the other hand, we have no very adequate vocabulary for discussing idiom.

Similarly, the structure of poetry differs in different languages. In English, rhythm depends on stress; in French, the number of syllables is what counts, and English people (including myself) generally put far too much stress into French poetry when reading it aloud. In Greek and Latin verse the pattern is made up of long and short syllables. This is known as *quantity* (a false quantity being the lengthening or shortening of a vowel incorrectly). In English, we cannot really speak of long or short syllables; some vowels are longer than others, other things being equal, so that 'man' is shorter than 'moon', but stress is much more important, and length may be considerably affected by stress: for instance, a vowel in an unstressed syllable frequently becomes a neutral vowel in ordinary rapid speech.[1] Quantitative verse is verse in which the pattern is made by arrangements of long or short syllables; attempts have been made by poets who were also classical scholars to write English quantitative verse; examples may be found in the works of Sidney, Spenser, Campion, Tennyson and Clough; but the results have never been encouraging, since no fixed rules for English 'quantities' can be made and we have to read English quantitative verse in a rather artificial manner if the pattern is to be preserved. Such verse can be no more than a technical exercise. For this reason the breve and macron are not at all suitable for the analysis of English rhythms, and all our usual metrical terms, such as *iambic*,

[1] For a full account of the phonetics of English, Ida Ward's *The Phonetics of English* (Heffer, 6s.) is very useful.

trochaic and *dactylic*, being taken from the terminology of quantitative verse, are not ideal for English. Perhaps some day a terminology more suitable to our native tongue will be invented. Robert Bridges, a great prosodist, tried to popularize the terms 'Rising' and 'Falling' Rhythm.[1] These terms fulfil a real want but have never captured the fancy of teachers. I shall use the classical terms in this book, for they are constantly used in textbooks and critical works and are wanted for examinations; but I am not satisfied with them, and would like to warn the student to be very careful not to apply them without sufficient thought.

When we examine some verses, we notice that a kind of pattern of stresses runs through them. It is not the whole of the rhythm; if this repetitive pattern were the whole, some trivial doggerel from a women's magazine would be more 'correct' poetry than most of Milton or Shakespeare; but the pattern is there to be heard. In English, we generally have all strong stresses separated by one unstressed syllable between them, or more than one.[2] This happens in common speech:

How do you do? I hope you are feeling better to-day?

If every syllable were stressed, speech would be both monotonous and exhausting, since stress is produced by putting more force of breath to the syllable. The *metre* of poetry is *the basic pattern of stressed and unstressed syllables.*

[1] Robert Bridges: *Milton's Prosody* (O.U.P.). A most stimulating and enlightening book which should be better known among nonspecialists.

[2] 'Stressed' syllables are stressed only in relation to other syllables. Minor variations of the intensity of stress are infinite.

If a line of poetry begins with a stressed syllable, the pattern will run something thus:

Mínnehàha, Láughing Wáter. . . .

or, perhaps:

Táke her up ténderly,
Líft her with cáre. . . .

and the effect will be 'falling', as Bridges calls it. The first pattern is called TROCHAIC, and may be described as alternating stressed and unstressed syllables, beginning with a stressed syllable. The second is called DACTYLIC, and may be described as alternating one stressed and two unstressed syllables, beginning with a stressed syllable. (Those who knit will know that when we are doing 'knit one, purl one' it does matter very much whether we begin the row with a knit or purl stitch.) It will be noticed that in the example of dactylic pattern chosen there is a stressed syllable at the end of the second line, without the two unstressed syllables that might be expected. This omission of final unstressed syllables often happens in the two main 'falling' rhythms, since there are relatively few English words that would fit the complete rhythm. More will be said about these variations, often wrongly called irregularities, in the next chapter.

The commonest kind of English metre has a pattern something like this:

Thát tíme of yéar thou máy'st in mé behóld. . . .

—a pattern alternating stressed and unstressed syllables beginning with an unstressed syllable. This is called IAMBIC. It is found, with five stresses to a line, in all the plays of Shake-

23

speare, all heroic couplets, all sonnets, *Paradise Lost*, *The Faerie Queen*, *Idylls of the King* and many other of our best-known poems; iambic metre is also the basis of many other well-known English verse forms. As it happens, the commonest variation in iambic verse is to invert the order of the stresses in the first group, so the student who is looking for iambic rhythm should be careful to pick it up by ear rather than by arithmetic. Even in the line above, chosen for its regularity, I am not at all sure that it might not be better to put the stress on the first rather than the second word.

The last metre that is at all common in English is the ANAPAESTIC, a pattern in which one stressed syllable alternates with two unstressed syllables, but beginning with the two unstressed syllables, as:

The Assyrian came down like a wolf on the fold. . . .

It will be noticed that this gives a feeling of urgent movement.

Certain other terms borrowed from classical prosody are sometimes used in describing English verse, but, though it could be argued that such feet are found in English, lines following these basic patterns are not found. These are: Spondee (two stressed syllables together), Amphibrach (unstressed-stressed-unstressed), Amphimacer or Cretic (stressed-unstressed-stressed) and Pyrrhic (two unstressed). The student of English poetry only may sometimes find the term Spondee useful to comment on a particular line, but is never likely to want the other terms.

When we analyse the basic pattern or *metre* of a poem, we first decide upon the basic pattern (iambic, trochaic, anapaestic or dactylic) and then divide it into FEET to give the type of line. The safest way to divide a line into feet is to count the stressed syllables first; in the basic pattern there are as many feet as stressed syllables, and the 'foot' is the stressed syllable together with the unstressed syllables that naturally attach themselves to it. (If there seem to be some syllables 'left over', they should probably be 'left over' at the end of the line rather than at the beginning.) Scansion, however, is a matter of cultivating the ear rather than learning fixed rules, for the basic pattern is never found for long without variations, and the student who tries to treat scansion as an aspect of arithmetic is sure to be seriously misled sooner or later.

The number of feet in a line is important. Obviously, a short line has fewer feet than a long one. For those who like a lot of technical terms, or are expected to make use of them, here are the terms for lines of various lengths:

Seven feet (very rare)	SEPTENARIUS
Six feet	HEXAMETER (This is also the name of a common classical metre)
Five feet (our com- monest line)	PENTAMETER
Four feet	TETRAMETER (*not* Quadruped!)
Three feet	TRIMETER
Two feet	DIMETER
One foot (rare)	MONOMETER.

Thus in the examples given above the first is TROCHAIC TETRA-METER, the first line of the second a DACTYLIC DIMETER, the third example an IAMBIC PENTAMETER, and the fourth an ANAPAESTIC TETRAMETER. These terms sound very dull, but it is sometimes convenient to know them.[1]

[1] May an experienced examiner warn readers that all the words describing the number of feet in a line end in -METER, and that the basic pattern is METRE? the difference is a fruitful cause of irritating misspellings.

Here are four little helps to memory for the student who is liable to confuse the four main basic English metres:

> Iambic feet are firm and flat
> And come down heavily like THAT.

> Trochees dancing very lightly
> Sparkle, froth and bubble brightly.

> Dactylic daintiness lilting so prettily
> Moves about fluttering rather than wittily.

> While for speed and for haste such a rhythm is the best
> As we find in the race of the quick anapaest.

When we have learned to recognize these customary basic patterns, we may be tempted to think that we know all about the rhythm of poetry. In fact, the most interesting part, which is yet to come, is more important and is often ignored.

IV. RHYTHM

(B) VARIATION: COUNTERPOINT

Change is the nursery
Of musicke, joy, life and eternity.
DONNE: *Elegy III*

I F we try to work out the rhythm of a poem merely by counting syllables, tapping our fingers on the table or repeating the lines in the monotonous and murderous 'ke-bonk, ke-bonk' fashion, we shall soon find ourselves in difficulties. Let us take a favourite line from Shakespeare:

To be or not to be, that is the question. . . .

We may think (rightly) that Shakespeare's basic verse pattern was the iambic pentameter, and, ke-bonking happily on the desk, produce the following monstrosity:

To bé or nót to bé, that ís the quéstion.

If we know our technical terms, we then say that this is a regular iambic pentameter line except for one extra unstressed syllable at the end. The scholar may object that there are probably two unstressed syllables at the end, as -ion endings were often pronounced i-on in Shakespeare's day. This does not much matter; but if we try to speak the line as our mechanical stresses indicate, we soon realize that it is completely unnatural and very ugly. A Hamlet who talked thus would be pelted off the stage. If we stress the line as the thought in it suggests, it will probably be something like this:

To bé or nót to be, thát is the quéstion

with rather less stress on 'quest-' than on the other stressed syllables. *What* is troubling Hamlet is the problem of whether to *live* or to *die*; these, the important ideas, should dictate the stresses.

If we turn back to the example of dactylic metre in Chapter III, we find:

Take her up ténderly,

Líft her with cáre.

The first line is 'regular'; in the second, we have a dactylic foot of perfect 'regularity' followed by a single stressed syllable. To speak of this as an 'irregularity', as if it were a carelessness on the part of the poet, is stupid; carelessness would be ugly. The effect of this is beautiful and adds to the feeling of gentle regret, the 'dying fall' suitable to the pathetic theme of a young girl's suicide. Dactylic metre in English generally has some incomplete feet, as the number of dactylic words in English is small, and, if the line is to end with a rhyme-word, a whole word is needed for the last foot, rather than a mono-syllable followed by two unimportant words. In classical pro-sody a line which has an 'extra' syllable or syllables is called a line with *hypermetric* syllables and a line which has a syllable short is called *catalectic*. It is also possible for a whole foot to be *hypermetric*. These terms can be applied to English versifica-tion and the student may find it convenient to be able to recognize them, though there is probably no need to make the effort to learn them.

If we take the line from *Hamlet* as it is stressed in natural speech, according to the meaning, we must describe it something like this:

'Iambic pentameter, with an unstressed third foot, inversion of the fourth foot and one or possibly two hypermetric syllables after the last foot.'

We might add, if we were being very minute in our description:

'The strongest stress in the line is on the stressed syllable of the inverted fourth foot.'

'Regularity,' in the sense of each foot being exactly like the next and each line being exactly like the next, would be not a merit but a defect in poetry. Most people not poets, when they try to write verses, find it difficult to make them 'scan' unless they have a natural ear for rhythm, but a series of completely 'regular' lines would be, not a proof of poetic skill, but unbearably monotonous. I have written a short example of perfectly regular iambic pentameters; the subject is suggested by the Domestic Science College in which I am at present lecturing:

A student sat and sewed with crimson thread
A brightly coloured quilt to deck a bed;
The work was wearing out her tired eyes
And so, although she hoped to win a prize,
She let her sewing fall, began to stare

At what she saw through windows; trees now bare,
A thrush that seemed too cold and sad to fly,
A curve of huge and grey and gloomy sky,
A corner piece of uninspiring wall.
She heard the bell and hastened towards the hall.

I think it will be agreed that these lines, though not ungrammatical and not without some meaning, are very dull to read, and that it is impossible to read them aloud without a childish sing-song. There are five stresses in each line, and the arrangement is mathematically regular. Let us now see what happens when the words are altered, changing the meaning as little as possible but injecting a few irregularities into the basic metre:

A student sat, sewing with crimson thread	inversion, 3rd foot
A brightly coloured quilt to deck a bed;	
The tiring work was trying to her eyes,	4th weak
So, though she hoped to win a certain prize,	1st inverted
She let her sewing fall, began to stare	
Out of the window, at the trees, now bare,	1st inverted; 3rd weak
At a cold thrush, too cold and sad to fly,	1st weak, 2 stresses in 2nd
A huge grey curve of dull and gloomy sky,	2 stresses in 2nd
A bit of uninspiring architecture;	hypermetric syllable at end, giving a feminine rhyme
She heard the bell and hurried to her lecture.	as above; 4th weak

I have deliberately written some trivial verse for this experiment, as it would be sacrilege to alter some fine poem to demonstrate the importance of variation. Yet the reader will probably agree that the second version sounds more natural and lively. Even the crude variations in this crude verse have some effect: the feminine rhyme comes as a surprise which is, I hope, amusing; 'tiring' and 'trying' is an internal partial rhyme; 'out' is emphasized, and the 'cold thrush' and 'huge grey curve' are made more oppressive by the extra stress given to them.

Shakespeare plays this trick with genius instead of crudity, as in the lovely, haunting line:

Bare ruined choirs, where late the sweet birds sang.

There is also a lighter stress on 'birds', making the line a very heavy and melancholy one.

It will be seen from the above examples that the main possibilities of varying the basic metre of a poem are: leaving one foot without a strong stress (a weak foot); putting two strong stresses in one foot; putting a hypermetric syllable at the end of a line or elsewhere; inverting any foot. These variations can be practised on all the basic patterns.

The function of the basic metre is to provide a regular undercurrent, a kind of pulse-beat of the poem, over which the interesting variations are heard. Unless we recognize the basic metre, by ear at least, not necessarily by name, we cannot appreciate the variations. What happens when we hear a poem and like the rhythm is that we quickly (probably after the first line) learn to expect a repetition of this pattern; we keep receiving small shocks of different kinds, which are pleasurable. At least, they are pleasurable in the work of a good poet! If they are not, we are roused to protest that the verses 'do not scan'. It is most unfortunate that many people have had so narrow a concept of 'rhythm' forced upon them that they feel a poem 'does not scan' if it contains variations, and therefore try to force it into unnatural, ugly rhythms if it is the work of an acknowledged master, or condemn it as incompetent if it is by a poet unlucky enough to be still alive! I am not myself musical, but have been told that these variations in poetry fulfil a function much like that of counterpoint in music. Perhaps it is also possible to compare these variations with the tiny variations in handmade lace or knitting which make it more attractive than machine-made goods, so much so that I am told machines have been devised to provide the appearance of human irregularities in machine-made goods! Other analogies may be drawn from our everyday experience. In marriage, a husband or wife is expected to be faithful, loyal and reliable; but marriages in which routine is all-important and neither spouse ever seeks to give a pleasant surprise to the other or to do something gay and impulsive are not very successful. We wish to have steady, trustworthy friends; we take pleasure in their habits and customs, their personal repetitions, but we all like to have friends who are also interesting and sometimes surprise us with original ideas, or do unusual things. We enjoy going for a walk along the same lane many times; but, while part of the pleasure is in the familiarity, part lies in the new discoveries at different seasons and in different weathers. It could well be argued that all personal life, all human history, consists of basic patterns on which variations are superimposed. In skilfully written poetry, the variations on the basic metre generally coincide with important words or with changes of emotion. Shakespeare is full of magnificent examples of this; the marriage of metrical to emotional change is obviously more valuable in dramatic even than in lyrical poetry.

When Romeo is about to poison himself over what he believes to be the dead body of Juliet, he says:

> O! here
> Will I set up my everlasting rest
> And shake the yoke of inauspicious stars
> From this world-wearied flesh. Eyes, look your last!

In this last line there are two stresses in the fourth foot, emphasizing Romeo's resolve to die and making the pathos of the last farewell more solemn. Another beautiful effect achieved by the variation of the fourth foot is to be found in *The Winter's Tale*, this time in a happy context. Hermione meets her daughter, Perdita, who has been lost for sixteen years. She greets her thus:

> You gods, look down
> And from your sacred vials pour your graces
> Upon my daughter's head! Tell me, mine own,
> Where hast thou been preserved?

How tender and urgent in its emphasis is that inverted fourth foot, 'Tell me . . .'. To stress the basic pattern here and say 'Tell *me*' would be obviously absurd, since no one else is asking Perdita to tell her story.

Out of weakness, too, a line can be made strong; one of the strongest lines in *Othello* has only three stressed syllables, thus throwing great emphasis on to those syllables:

> It is the cáuse, it is the cáuse, my soúl!

At the other end of the scale, Milton makes one line from

Paradise Lost heavy and impressive by loading with stressed syllables:

/   /   /   /   /   /   /
Rocks, Caves, Lakes, Fens, Bogs, Dens, and shades
                        /
                      of Death,

in which lines the first three feet are spondees!
In a lighter context, Viola in *Twelfth Night* says:

None of my lord's ring! why, he sent her none!

where the inversion of the first foot emphasizes 'none' and suggests an intonation of surprise; the two stresses in the third foot clash together; she is answering her own question. In *Much Ado about Nothing*, when Leonato is outraged by the supposed unchastity of his innocent daughter, he says fiercely:

For, did I think thou wouldst not quickly die,
Thought I thy spirits were stronger than thy shames,
Myself would, on the rearward of reproaches,
Strike at thy life. Griev'd I, I had but one?

The first line is more or less 'regular'; the next line has a hypermetric syllable, and this time it is not at the end of the line, which is a firm monosyllable of emphatic meaning, but must be taken as the second syllable of either 'spirits' or 'stronger'; this stumble in the middle of the line helps to suggest Leonato's mental distress. The next line has another hypermetric syllable, this time at the end; the second and fourth feet are both inverted, making a very loose line; this leads up to the shock of the next foot, 'Strike at', which is inverted to give it additional force. In this line we then have an inversion of the third foot which emphasizes 'Griev'd'. We can take any play of Shakespeare's at random and speedily find a number of interesting examples of the way in which these variations, standing out in contrast to an underlying basic pattern, give dramatic point and emphasis to particular words. Indeed, some of Shakespeare's acknowledge superiority to his contemporaries lies in his use of rhythm for dramatic purposes. For instance, almost all Marlowe's lines, even in his finest passages, are stopped at the end; Shakespeare's, in which the sense of one line frequently runs over into the next, are more flexible.[1] If we read Shakespeare's plays in approximate chronological order, we see how he moved away from the end-stopped line to a more flexible line. The dramatists of the Jacobean period are even more flexible in their verse rhythms, so much so that they sometimes lose the basic pattern and stumble into a kind of half-verse, half-prose. Here is a passage from Webster's *The Duchess of Malfi* in which the variations add to the pathos:

Verse	Scansion notes
Oh, that it were possible we might	1st foot strong, 2nd weak 4th weak
But hold some two days' conference with the dead!	3rd strong, 4th weak
From them I should learn somewhat, I am sure,	4th weak
I never shall know here. I'll tell thee a miracle;	Hypermetric syllable in 5th & 2 more at end
I am not mad yet, to my cause of sorrow;	1st weak, 2nd strong 3rd weak hypermetric syllable at end.
The heaven o'er my head seems made of molten brass,	2nd weak; one extra foot
The earth of flaming sulphur, yet I am not mad	Extra and strong foot

[1] The technical term for this 'running over' is ENJAMBEMENT.

/   /   / /
I am acquainted with sad misery   3rd weak
/   /   /   /   /
As the tann'd galley-slave is with his oar;   1st inverted
                                    2nd strong
   /   /   /   /   3rd weak
Necessity makes me suffer constantly   Hypermetric in
     /   /   /   2nd
And custom makes it easy.

This play was first published in 1623. In this passage there is so much variation that at times we seem to lose the undercurrent of the iambic beat. This might elsewhere be a fault; variation carried to the point that there is nothing on which to have a variation is obviously useless; but in this context the looseness of the verse has a strange, touching beauty; after long mental torment, the Duchess is still resisting madness, and the touch of verbal and metrical incoherence suggests how near to it she has come; the madmen who enter presently speak in prose.

Here I will mention the *Theory of Equivalence*, an important development in the history of English prosody, and one to which the student may find allusions. It is also sometimes called the *Theory of Substitution*, and is another way of expressing what I have been trying to explain, depending rather more on those concepts of classical prosody which are no longer a part of the information of every educated person. It is discussed in detail, with a rich store of interesting examples, in George Saintsbury's *Manual of English Prosody*, a book which every student who becomes seriously interested in verse forms ought to read. (It is rather solid for an inexperienced student.) According to the theory of substitution, one kind of foot may be substituted for another equivalent foot; an iambic foot may be replaced somewhere in a line by a trochaic or anapaestic foot, a trochaic foot replaced by a dactyl and so on; it must not take place so often that the basic metre is lost. Even Saintsbury, with his immense erudition, had to admit that the experience of the human ear, rather than a fixed rule, showed whether in a given line a substitution was acceptable. What I call an 'inverted iambic foot' Saintsbury would have called a 'substituted equivalent trochee'.

So far we have studied metre and variation chiefly in dramatic blank verse. Variation will be more common in the best dramatic verse than in non-dramatic verse, because, as I hope I have shown, it plays a part in the actual dramatic effect. However, examples may be found throughout the mass of English lyric poetry. Here are a few lines from Andrew Marvell's *The Garden*:

> How vainly men themselves amaze
> To win the palm, the oak, or bays,
> And their incessant labours see
> Crowned from some single herb or tree,
> Whose short and narrow-verged shade
> Does prudently their toils upbraid;
> While all flowers and all trees do close
> To weave the garland of repose.

The first two lines are completely 'regular', to enable the reader to grasp the basic pattern of iambic tetrameter. The first foot in the third line is weak, leading up effectively to the stress on 'Crowned', an emphatic inversion. The next conspicuous variation is in line 7, an oddly beautiful line in its rhythmical context. I think it should be scanned:

> While áll flówers and áll trées do clóse.

Here we have two feet inverted, or two substituted equivalent trochees, with a strange effect of wonder in the natural intonation. In the next line there is only one inversion.

Often in lyrical poetry, especially short lyrics, substitution or variation is such that the effect is of a mixed metre. This is not the mere loss of the basic metre in confusion, which would sound like bad prose and be slovenly writing, but must, I think, be taken as an example of what is common in classical metres, a basic line pattern made up of more than one kind of foot. A pretty example is the well-known song from John Gay's *Acis and Galatea*:

> O ruddier than the cherry,
> O sweeter than the berry,
> O Nymph more bright
> Than moonshine night,
> Like kidlings blithe and merry.
> Ripe as the melting cluster,
> No lily has such lustre,
> Yet hard to tame
> As raging flame
> And fierce as storms that bluster.

The basic metre of this poem would seem, if we look at the four short lines, to be iambic, but in all the other lines, though the basis is iambic, the last foot has a hypermetric syllable making a feminine rhyme. This is so much a part of the structure that the basic metre of the poem might be said to be iambic-plus-trochaic, or perhaps, from the terminology of Bridges, a rising rhythm with a falling conclusion. Perhaps this is being over-pedantic, but I think we should have a distion between sporadic and systematic variation. Perhaps if we had not taken all our metrical terms from the classics we should have found a better way of expressing this!

A student working with me was once greatly puzzled by the rhythm of Tennyson's *Break, break, break*. The student should try to work it out before reading my analysis, as a test! Here is the poem with the lines numbered for easy reference later:

1 Break, break, break
2 On thy cold gray stones, O sea!
3 And I would that my tongue could utter
4 The thoughts that arise in me.

5 O well for the fisherman's boy,
6 That he shouts with his sister at play!
7 O well for the sailor lad,
8 That he sings in his boat on the bay!

9 And the stately ships go on
10 To their haven under the hill;
11 But O for the touch of a vanished hand
12 And the sound of a voice that is still!

13 Break, break, break,
14 At the foot of thy crags, O Sea!
15 But the tender grace of a day that is dead
16 Will never come back to me.

We can probably hear a pattern in this poem long before we can say what the basic metre is. It is one of those poems in which the rhythm is so delicate and complex that any attempt to 'ke-bonk' it into a regular pattern would mislead more than in a more regular poem. It is necessary to read the poem aloud, intelligently, and mark the syllables that are naturally stressed, remembering that equal stress is not laid on all stressed syllables. The basic metre of this poem is anapaestic, strange as this may seem in view of its slow, melancholy rhythm. Completely regular anapaestic trimeters are found in lines 6, 8, and

12, and nearly regular ones with only one unstressed syllable missing in lines 5, 10, and 14. Lines 11 and 15 also have unmistakably the anapaestic beat, but each, a tetrameter, has one iambic foot. Eight puzzling lines remain: the two pathetic repetitions of 'Break, break, break . . .' I would read as three almost equal strong stresses, making a very heavy line for the mood of mourning. Lines 2, 4, 7, and 16, have each three stresses, with a mixture of iambic and anapaestic feet. The effect of these complicated variations is to give a faltering effect to the poem, which well suggests by its sound the emotion it portrays.

Tennyson was a brilliant conscious artist. William Blake was an inexpert rather than a subtle prosodist; believing his poems to be literally and directly inspired, he seldom polished them as most poets do. Here is a short poem of indisputable beauty and power, which is, however, as enigmatic rhythmically as symbolically:

> O Rose, thou art sick!
>
> The invisible worm
>
> That flies in the night
>
> In the howling storm,
>
> Has found out thy bed
>
> Of crimson joy
>
> And his dark secret love
>
> Does thy life destroy.

This poem is almost too short to give us the sense of expectation that a basic metre would provide. It begins with three lines in the same rhythm, an iambic foot followed by an anapaest; the order is then reversed for two lines; the first pattern reappears in the last line (which rather suggests that it may be taken as the basic metre of the poem); the seventh line is anything but easy to describe. It seems to me to have four stresses, closely packed and sinister in tone. This poem implies by its very rhythm a kind of profoundly wise *naïveté*, although the suitability of the rhythm may not be intentional.

Many more examples could be cited for all our purposes, but perhaps enough have been discussed to show that the rhythms of poetry are not a matter of tapping mechanically on a desk or counting syllables on our fingers. Quite often it is possible to have a difference of opinion, not only on how the arrangement of stresses in a poem should be described, but on where the actual stresses are to be placed; otherwise the only differences in the interpretation of poems when spoken by different people would lie in the quality of the voices, and it is common experience that this is not so. Indeed, a certain ambiguity of rhythm is one of the beauties of a poem.[1] Sincerity is as important in the study of rhythm as in any other literary study, and any attempt to force the words into a too symmetrical pattern outrages the healthy ear.

[1] Mrs. Anne Ridler has a brilliant essay on this subject, so far unpublished; it is to be hoped that it will soon be available.

V. PHONETIC FORM

(A) RHYME

Where'er you find *the cooling western breeze*,
In the next line, it *whispers through the trees*;
If crystal streams *with pleasing murmurs creep*,
The reader's threaten'd (not in vain) with *sleep*.

POPE: *An Essay on Criticism*

SOME years ago I was walking along a country lane with a friend; we were trying to string some verses together; and my friend, who had a lively mind but no talent for verse composition, struggled with a promising first line until, giving up in despair, she convulsed us both by exclaiming: 'But I can't get a worm to ride!'

'A worm to ride' is the first thing the beginner in verse-writing seeks and is also the easiest part of the physical form of poetry to study. It is a repetition of some arrangement of vowels and consonants at the ends of lines, or sometimes in the middle, and is defined by H. W. Fowler in *Modern English Usage* as 'identity of sounds between words or lines extending back from the end to the last fully accented vowel and not farther'. Thus a rhyme-word may in theory have one, two, three, four or more syllables, though in practice, in serious poetry, rhymes of more than two syllables are rare. One-syllable rhymes may be called masculine, though there is seldom any need for the term; two-syllable rhymes, e.g. nation-station, are called feminine. If we wish to describe any other kind of rhyme we can use the words trisyllabic and poly-syllabic, there being no other special terms.

The student who has read attentively so far will see that feminine rhymes may be expected in trochaic verse or as a variation (a last foot with a hypermetric syllable) in iambic verse; masculine rhymes will be found in iambic verse or as variations (catalectic) in trochaic verse. Many different arrange-ments of rhymes are possible, from the extreme simplicity of the old ballads:

> I'll do as much for my true love
> As any young man may;
> I'll sit and mourn all at her grave
> For a twelvemonth and a day.

to the extreme elaboration of, say, Spenser's *Prothalamion*:

> Calm was the day, and through the trembling air
> Sweet-breathing zephyrus did softly play
> A gentle spirit, that lightly did delay
> Hot Titan's beams, which then did glister fair;
> When I (whom sullen care,
> Through discontent of my long fruitless stay
> In Prince's court, and expectation vain
> On idle hopes, which still do fly away,
> Like empty shadows, did afflict my brain.)
> Walked forth to ease my pain.
> Along the shore of silver streaming Thames;
> Whose rutty bank, the which his river hems,
> Was painted all with variable flowers,
> And all the meads adorned with dainty gems

Fit to deck maidens' bowers
And crown their paramours
Against their bridal day, which is not long:
Sweet Thames! run softly till I end my song.

It is customary and convenient to denote patterns of rhyme (commonly called 'rhyme-schemes') briefly by using letters of the alphabet; thus, the first example may be described as abcb and the second as abbaabcbccddedeeff. (We might also describe the first as abab; the matter of imperfect rhyme will be discussed later.) A detailed account of the common English rhyme-schemes with their usual names will be found in Chapter XV; for the present the student will be wise not to attempt to learn many of them.

The rhyme-scheme of a poem plays a part in its emotional effect, though not generally so great a part as the rhythm. The elaborate rhyme-scheme of Spenser's *Prothalamion* in itself suggests something formal, ceremonious and processional. Narrative is usually written in some fairly simple rhyme-scheme, such as the couplet (many of Chaucer's *Canterbury Tales*, Keats's *Lamia*, Scott's *Marmion*, Shelley's *The Sensitive Plant* and Byron's *The Prisoner of Chillon*) or the simple quatrain rhyming abcb or abab, as in the old ballads and later imitations of them such as Coleridge's *The Ancient Mariner*.[1] Sometimes, however, a more elaborate verse form is used for narrative, the most remarkable example being the difficult nine-line Spenserian stanza used in Spenser's *The Faerie Queene*; other complicated stanza forms for narrative may be found in Keats's *Isabella*, Byron's *Don Juan*, Shelley's *The Revolt of Islam* and many of the narrative poems of Robert Browning.

---

[1] The latter poem has also some internal rhymes and variations on the rhyme-scheme; these are occasionally found in the old ballads.

44

A narrative using one of the more complicated verse forms will move more slowly, in general, than one in a simpler form; it will contain less action and more description or reflection.

Satire demands a crisp rhyme-scheme, in which the unkind remarks follow one another rapidly, without fumbling. Heroic couplets, that is iambic pentameter couplets, are a favourite form for satire, as in Byron's *The Age of Bronze*:

> The *landed interest*—(you may understand
> The phrase much better leaving out the *land*)
> The land self-interest groans from shore to shore
> For fear that plenty should attain the poor.
> Up, up, again, ye rents! exalt your notes,
> Or else the ministry will lose their votes,
> And patriotism, so delicately nice,
> Her loaves will lower to the market price.

Thousands of different rhyme-schemes are possible for short lyrics, depending on the mood; alternations of long and short lines add to the variety. A very short lyric may not repeat a rhyme-scheme at all, but be, as it were, one verse; many of the Elizabethan madrigals are like this:

> Faustina hath the fairer face,
> And Phillida the feater grace;
> Both have mine eye enriched.
> This sings full sweetly with her voice,
> Her fingers make as sweet a noise;
> Both have mine ear bewitched.
> Ay me! sith Fates have so provided,
> My heart, alas! must be divided.

> ANONYMOUS, from *Airs and Madrigals*, 1598

More often a short poem repeats a verse form once, if only once:

> When to her lute Corinna sings,
> Her voice revives the leaden strings,
> And doth in highest notes appear
> As any challenged echo clear.
> But when she doth of mourning speak,
> Even with her sighs the strings do break.
>
> And as her lute doth live or die,
> Led by her passion, so must I.
> For when of pleasure she doth sing,
> My thoughts enjoy a sudden spring;
> But if she doth of sorrow speak,
> E'en from my heart the strings do break.

THOMAS CAMPION

The actual repetition of the verse form is part of the symmetry of a poem, and has perhaps something the same effect as parallelism in prose, as in 'He hath put down the mighty from their seats, and He hath exalted the humble and meek'.

The vast majority of English poems until the twentieth century have rhymes of one syllable, if they rhyme at all, blank verse (unrhymed iambic pentameter) having long been a favourite English form. Feminine rhymes, less common, trip rather more lightly:

> Trip no further, pretty sweeting;
> Journeys end in lovers meeting!

Poets quite often use masculine and feminine rhymes in alternation; this generally seems to produce a very melodious verse. Swinburne, a poet of more music than meaning at times, particularly favours this kind of rhyme-scheme:

From too much love of living,
From hope and fear set free,
We thank with brief thanksgiving
Whatever gods may be
That no life lives for ever;
That dead men rise up never;
That even the weariest river
Winds somewhere safe to sea.
                    The Garden of Proserpine

Thomas Hood uses an alternation of masculine and trisyllabic rhyme in the poem quoted in the third chapter:

Take her up tenderly,
Lift her with care;
Fashioned so slenderly,
Young, and so fair!
                    The Bridge of Sighs

Feminine rhymes are often used in humorous verse, in which they please by their witty ingenuity. The delight here is probably almost entirely in the pleasant shock of the unexpected. We wonder how the writer can possibly find a rhyme to the line we have just heard; but no—here it comes! The Puritans in Samuel Butler's *Hudibras* who

Compound for sins they are inclined to
By damning those they have no mind to   also
Quarrel with minced-pies, and disparage
Their best and dearest friend, plum-porridge;
Fat pig and goose itself oppose
And blaspheme custard through the nose.
The apostles of this fierce religion,
Like Mahomet's, were ass and widgeon

> To whom our Knight, by fast instinct
> Of wit and temper, was so linked,
> As if hypocrisy and nonsense
> Had got th'advowson of his conscience.

Rhymes of more than two syllables are very seldom used except with humorous intention, for they are so ingenious that we notice them as rhymes as well as an integral part of the verse form. Byron uses a good many multiple rhymes in *Don Juan*:

> Some women use their tongues—she *look'd* a lecture,
> Each eye a sermon, and her brow a homily,
> An all-in-all sufficient self-director,
> Like the lamented late Sir Samuel Romilly,
> The Law's expounder, and the State's corrector,
> Whose suicide was almost an anomaly—
> One sad example more than 'All is vanity'—
> The jury brought their verdict in 'Insanity'.

or

> I've got new mythological machinery
> And very handsome supernatural scenery.

When, in *Much Ado about Nothing*, Benedick is trying to write a poem for his lady-love, he can think of no rhyme for 'lady' but 'baby', no rhyme for 'school' but 'fool'. In *Romeo and Juliet* Mercutio invites Romeo to 'rhyme me but love and dove'. Evidently in Shakespeare's day poets were already conscious of the fact that some rhymes were hackneyed. The number of full rhymes to any word is limited; to many words in common use the number is very small. In humorous verse imperfect rhymes have sometimes been accepted, as in Byron's

> But they were mostly nervous six-foot fellows,
> All fit to make a Patagonian jealous.

and a few rhymes which are rhymes to the eye rather than the ear, such as *love* and *move*, have long been permitted by convention. In the twentieth century, however, the possibilities of rhyme in English have been given new life by the acceptance of several kinds of partial rhyme. This seems to me to be one of the most important developments in form in poetry, because it releases poets at one stroke from a dependence on habits of rhyme now so hackneyed that they restrict even the ideas that can be conveyed in verse. Wilfred Owen seems to have been the originator of this new technique; his editor, Edmund Blunden, calls Owen's partial rhymes *pararhymes*, a useful term which deserves to be more popular. If we read the small volume of the poems of Wilfred Owen, it is quite clear that he did not use pararhymes because he was lazy or careless or had a bad ear; they are woven into patterns as accurately and formally as the full rhymes of older poets, and he uses full rhymes with confidence. Here is the beginning of his fine poem, *Strange Meeting*:

> It seemed that out of battle I escaped,
> Down some profound dull tunnel, long since scooped
> Through granites which titanic wars had groined.
> Yet also there encumbered sleepers groaned,
> Too fast in thought or death to be bestirred.
> Then, as I probed them, one sprang up and stared
> With pitiless recognition in fixed eyes,
> Lifting distressful hands as if to bless.
> And by his smile, I knew that sullen hall,
> By his dead smile I knew we stood in Hell.

Generally, Wilfred Owen keeps an exact parallel in the consonants, and changes only the vowel sounds, but there are a
few exceptions to this:

Since we believe not otherwise can kind fires burn
Nor ever suns smile on child, or field, or *fruit*.
For God's invincible spring our love is made *afraid*;
Therefore, not loath, we lie out there; therefore we were born,
For love of God seems dying.

Many poets of the present day use pararhymes like Owen's.
Auden, for example, uses them a great deal. Pararhymes are
perhaps appropriate to the present, as they give an impression
of rather less certainty than full rhymes, and the present age is,
as Auden named it, the Age of Anxiety, full of hopes, fears
and vague ideas. Here is an example of pararhymes from
Auden; it will be noticed that the first rhyme in the verse is a
full rhyme:

> Wrapped in a yielding air, beside
> The flower's soundless hunger,
> Close to the tree's clandestine tide,
> Close to the bird's high fever,
> Loud in his hope and anger,
> Erect about his skeleton,
> Stands the expressive lover,
> Stands the deliberate man.

Assonance, also used by many good contemporary poets, is
the rhyming of vowel sounds without regard for the consonants, as in Louis MacNeice's:

Not the twilight of the gods but a precise dawn
Of sallow and grey bricks, and the newsboys crying war.

Another kind of partial rhyme is what I would like to call *Semi-Rhyme*, in which an unstressed syllable follows the rhyming or pararhyming syllable in one word but not in both, as in sun, running; toad, roaming; it is also possible to have what might perhaps be called an *Unaccented Rhyme*, in which one of the rhyme-syllables is a stressed syllable but the other is not, as in Robert Penn Warren's *Original Sin*:

> But it has not died, it comes, its hand childish,
> >   unsure,
> Clutching the bribe of chocolate or a toy you used to
> >   treasure.

or in George Fraser's *Two Sonnets*:

> The intricacy of the exposed intestines
> Present no easy formal inspiration
> Till art disguises them as wreathing vines.

(It is evident from the two poems from which these lines are taken that the unaccented rhymes are intended to serve as rhymes.)

Gerard Manley Hopkins, whose daring of technique has had an enormous influence on contemporary poetry, occasionally uses what might be called a *Suspended Rhyme*, in which the rhyme is made by borrowing a sound from the following line:

> But what black Boreas *wrecked her? he*
> Came equipped, deadly-*electric*. . . .

Only the force of his genius can allow Hopkins to risk this rather ugly distortion, though it is considerably less offensive to the ear than to the eye.

The student who is confined to poetry before 1914 probably need not pay much attention to the new types of rhyme; but to me it seems entirely wrong that any student of English poetry should neglect our own contemporaries. They are the only poets whose poetry can be nourished and drawn out by our encouragement, or stunted by our neglect, and the great living are even more a part of a nation's glory than the great dead. Moreover, the serious student of poetry will want to keep up with the times and understand the new technical problems and the solutions found for them. All the new possibilities of rhyme increase the possibility of originality and interest in the poetry of the future, and may well prove to be very important in refreshing the tradition.

VI. PHONETIC FORM

(B) ONOMATOPOEIA

With a quack, quack, here, and a quack, quack, there,
Here a quack, there a quack, everywhere a quack, quack . . .
Old MacDougall

RHYTHM obviously helps a great deal in supporting the meaning of the words of a poem; but sometimes the sound of the words also gives great support to the sense. *Cool moonlight*, with long vowels and two l-sounds, certainly sounds more restful and still than *fidgetty kittens*, with short vowels and brittle t-sounds. This tendency in words to echo the meaning by the actual sound is called ONOMATO-POEIA.[1] It is found in an almost pure form in many of the words describing sounds, such as *buzz*, *fizz*, *crash*, *bang*, *thump*, *miaow*, *quack*, *giggle*, *sizzle*, *hiss*, *sneeze*, *thud*, *snort*, and even a long word such as *effervescence*. Sometimes we lose the onomatopoeic effect of words because we do not trouble to pronounce them properly; failing to open our mouths and move our lips and tongues as freely as we should, we turn a vigorous, expressive word into a dull and slovenly sound something like it. To hear a reciter of the calibre of Edith Evans, or Rachel Marshall of the Speech Fellowship, or an actor of the calibre of Sir Laurence Olivier, is to become aware

[1] The correct adjective is *onomatopoeic* or *onomatopoeical*.

53

of the possibilities of English sounds in a new way, for the majority of English people are far lazier in speaking their beautiful language than they would dream of being in washing their faces or writing a letter.

Onomatopoeia is very common in poetry, but it is difficult to know whether a poet is using it as a deliberate artistic effect or by accident, for so many English words are onomatopoeic that, if the poet chooses the right word in meaning, he is likely automatically to choose the onomatopoeic word. Blake, for example, who took relatively little trouble over technicalities, has such lines as:

> For the gentle wind does move
> Silently, invisibly. . . .

which sounds very quiet with its many l-sounds, f's and v's. And what could sound more bubbly and stream-like than his:

> But a Pebble of the brook
> Warbled out these metres meet

with its b's and r's? The answer to my question is Tennyson's *Brook*, for Tennyson, the more conscious artist and a master of onomatopoeia, gave his brook more of the b's and r's as well as some fluid-sounding l's:

> I chatter over stony ways
> In little sharps and trebles,
> I bubble into eddying bays,
> I babble on the pebbles.

It is not necessary to read this with any exaggeration in order to hear the brook doing all that it says it does. Here are a few more examples from Tennyson:

Slowness and peace suggested by the use of long vowels, l's, m's and n's:

> The long day wanes; the slow moon climbs; the deep
> Moans round with many voices.
>
> *Ulysses*

Three familiar country sounds:

> The sparrow's chirrup on the roof,
> The slow clock ticking, and the sound
> Which to the wooing wind aloof
> The poplar made. . . .
>
> *Mariana*

Peacefulness suggested by l's and many long vowels:

> Music that gentlier on the spirit lies
> Than tired eyelids upon tired eyes;
> Music that brings sweet sleep down from the blissful skies.
> Here are cool mosses deep,
> And through the moss the ivies creep,
> And in the streams the long-leaved flowers weep,
> And from the craggy ledge the poppy hangs in sleep.
>
> *The Lotos-Eaters*

Violence and splintering suggested by hard consonants and short vowels:

> Scarce had she ceased, when out of heaven a bolt
> (For now the storm was close above them) struck,
> Furrowing a giant oak, and javelining
> With darted spikes and splinters of the wood
> The dark earth round.
>
> *Merlin and Vivien*

Presently, too, Vivien in the thunderstorm is

> dazzled by the livid-flickering forks,
> And deafened by the stammering cracks and claps.

Violence is again to be found in:

> last a heathen horde,
> Reddening the sun with smoke and earth with blood,
> And on the spike that split the mother's heart
> Spitting the child. . . .   *The Coming of Arthur*

Pope was another poet with a great conscious awareness of the use of onomatopoeia. He refers to it as a very necessary part of a poet's technique:

> 'Tis not enough no harshness gives offence,
> The sound must seem an echo to the sense.
> Soft is the strain when Zephyr gently blows,
> And the smooth stream in smoother numbers flows;
> But when loud surges lash the sounding shore,
> The hoarse, rough verse should like the torrent roar.
> When Ajax strives, some rock's vast weight to throw,
> The line too labours, and the words move slow;
> Not so, when swift Camilla scours the plain,
> Flies o'er the unbending corn, and skims along the main.
> *An Essay on Criticism*

Onomatopoeic effects are cultivated with great skill by a number of contemporary poets, notably Vachel Lindsay, Dr. Edith Sitwell and Dylan Thomas. Poems containing many onomatopoeic effects are particularly suitable for reading aloud and for choral speaking. Onomatopoeia may attract us not only by the accuracy with which it gives a sound-picture of the things or events it describes, but also by lulling us into a trance as a kind of incantation. Vachel Lindsay has specialized

56

in this aspect of onomatopoeia in such poems as *The Congo*, *The Santa Fé Trail* and *The Ghosts of the Buffaloes*. Some of Dr. Sitwell's earliest poems are little more than wonderful patterns of sound such as have probably never been surpassed in their kind; the student will enjoy reading her *Trio for Two Cats and a Trombone*, *Three Poor Witches*, *The Wind's Bastinado*, *Country Dance*, *Hornpipe* and *Sir Beelzebub*. The reader who is seriously interested in the study of how particular speech sounds have particular mental effects can probably study nothing more helpful than Dr. Sitwell's *A Poet's Notebook* and her *Alexander Pope*.

It seems probable that at this stage in the history of our literature when criticism has come of age and almost every possible aspect of poetry has been analysed in minute detail— far more detail than is anywhere possible in this little book —poets are themselves using these sound effects more consciously than ever before. This is not necessarily a good thing; craftsmanship is not always great art and there are many occasions both in life and in literature when sincerity and spontaneity are more important than accuracy and scholarship. However, we cannot repudiate any knowledge we gain, and it will be interesting to see the further developments of poetry in this wonderfully fruitful and experimental era. It is extremely unlikely that many poets, having learned some facts about onomatopoeic effects from studying other poems, apply them with a formulated technique; the result would probably sound dull and laboured. The fact that the most suitable word is often also the onomatopoeically effective word depends on aspects of language so primitive that we are seldom conscious of them while we are using the words.

The student may like to read a few general hints on the effect of some speech sounds used onomatopoeically. These should not be taken as a statement of fact; the effect will depend very much on the context and the other sounds found in juxtaposition.

In general, long vowels tend to sound more peaceful or more solemn than short ones, which tend to give an impression of quick movement, agitation or triviality.

b *and* p	explosive sounds, suggest quickness, movement, triviality, scorn.
m, n, ng	provide various effects of humming, singing, music, occasionally sinister.
l	suggests liquids in motion, streams, water, rest, peace, luxury, voluptuousness.
k, g, st, ts, ch	suggest harshness, violence, cruelty, movement, discomfort, noise, conflict.
s, sh	hissing, also soft and smooth, soothing sounds. Robert Graves points out[1] that the correct manipulation of the letter S is important to a poet, for too many S's are over-conspicuous in a line. At all times a bad reader who prolongs s-sounds can spoil a poem.
z	tends to appear in contexts of harshness.
f, w	and to a lesser extent v, suggest wind, wings and any motion of a light and easy kind.
t, d	are like k, g, but less emphatic, and are much used in contexts where short actions are described.
r	more perhaps than the other sounds, depends on the sounds near it, but is generally found in contexts of movement and noise.
th	hard and soft, tends to be quiet and soothing.

[1] In *On English Poetry*.

Those who wish to analyse these effects in detail will find the study of Phonetics very helpful, both in suggesting ideas and in providing an unambiguous notation. I was tempted to use phonetic notation in this chapter, but it is apt to frighten beginners!

VII. PHONETIC FORM

(C) INTERNAL PATTERN

Whereat with blade, with bloody blameful blade,
He bravely broached his boiling bloody breast.
SHAKESPEARE: *A Midsummer Night's Dream*

S YMMETRY of form in a poem is achieved chiefly by
the rhythm-pattern and the rhyme-scheme, but, just
as a fine painting has a magnificent total form and yet
it is possible for a book on art to print a reproduction of a
'detail', one face or foot or tree, to show the skill of the artist,
so a poem can have details within the main structure. These
details include alliteration, all kinds of internal rhymes, asson-
ances, echoes and various kinds of repetition and contrast.
Many of these devices have long Greek names that no one uses
nowadays and that make no difference to our enjoyment or
admiration. An amusing example of the over-pedantic approach may be found in the 'Glosse' (notes) to Spenser's *The
Shepheards Calender*, in which Spenser's friend E.K. comments
on the lines

I love thilke lasse, (alas! why doe I love?)
And am forlorne, (alas! why am I lorne?)

thus: 'A prety Epanorthosis in these two verses; and withal a
Paranomasia or playing with the word. . . .' We can enjoy
the trivial prettiness of the trick without this help.

However, to have an ear for these internal patterns is to enjoy poetry more. Alliteration, one of the most generally used internal ornaments, was once the very basis of the physical form of English poetry. Anglo-Saxon poetry, the earliest English literature, includes poems written in alliterative verse, such as *Beowulf*, *The Dream of the Rood* and *The Battle of Maldon*, magnificent works of art which, for their merit, deserve to be much better known, but will probably never be well known even to the British, since Anglo-Saxon is quite a difficult language to learn and is of less practical use than Latin, Greek or Sanskrit, being a dead language without a continuing tradition.[1] To sum up the rules of Anglo-Saxon poetry in a very hasty manner, three words in each line had to begin with the same letter; there were patterns of rhythm obeying fairly strict rules, but no rhymes. The composers of these poems seem to have been highly conscious artists, for there are a number of allusions to the bard's 'word-hoard' and the need to 'wrestle with words'. This method of alliteration, known as 'head-rhyme', continued to be practised as late as the end of the fourteenth century with 'Langland's' great poem *The Vision of Piers Plowman*.[2] However, as soon as English poets had learned the method of rhyme from continental poets, alliteration became less important, sinking from being the essential feature of poetic structure to being a decora-

[1] Anglo-Saxon or Old English is the language used in England before 1066, and cannot be understood without learning it as a separate language. Middle English is the language used roughly 1066-1500 and can be understood with occasional reference to a glossary. The student who wishes to sample Anglo-Saxon literature without learning the language will find much delight in the excellent translations by Gavin Bone.

[2] The authorship of this work is much disputed.

tion. This must have made poetry more flexible, since it is easier to find one appropriate rhyme per line than to work out a series of lines each with three alliterating words.

Alliteration is near to being an instinctive method of emphasis; in Shaw's *Pygmalion* the phonetic expert Henry Higgins is rebuked by his housekeeper for applying a certain vulgar word to 'your boots, to the butter and to the brown bread', and excuses himself by saying: 'Oh! that! Mere alliteration, Mrs. Pearce, natural to a poet.' If we observe our own conversation, we may notice many alliterations. Many proverbial and idiomatic expressions gain much of their force from alliteration, for example: 'Fine feathers make fine birds'; 'All is not gold that glitters'; 'Speech is silvern, silence is golden.' We speak of something being in 'bits and bobs' or decked in 'buttons and bows'; we strive with 'might and main' to find something of which we have not lately seen 'hide or hair' and candidates at elections talk of 'peace and prosperity' rather than 'peace and wealth'.

Since alliteration plays such a part in common speech, it is probable that not all alliteration in poetry is deliberate; as with onomatopoeia, the words that are intellectually right tend also to be the words that are most attractive in sound. Christopher Smart was of doubtful sanity when he wrote *The Song to David*, with such charming alliterations as:

> *S*weet is the lily's *s*ilver bell,
> And *s*weet the *w*akeful tapers' *s*mell
> That *w*atch for early prayer.

> *W*alk, *w*ater, meditated *w*ild,
> And all the *b*loomy *b*eds.

> Precious the *r*uby's *b*lushing *b*laze
> And alba's *b*lest imperial *r*ays,

Blake, too, produced probably without conscious intent, effects like this:

> Sweet *s*leep, with *s*oft down, . . .
>
> *B*ring me my *b*ow of *b*urning gold!
>
> *W*eeping in *w*eak and mortal clay. . . .

When we turn to the more deliberately literary poets, we find a great deal of alliteration, often in very elaborate patterns, so that poetry almost becomes embroidery. There are no technical terms at present in general use for the different kinds of alliteration, but two types with rather different effects can be distinguished: one I will call *piled alliteration*, in which the initial letter is repeated several times to give a cumulative effect, and which is generally used for emphasis; the other has been called *crossed alliteration*, in which two or more initial letters are woven into a pattern, perhaps in alternation, to give a kind of balance. The second is by far the more subtle kind and probably the most attractive.

Piled alliteration for emphasis is to be found in facetious contexts, as in the motto to this chapter, and also in serious contexts, as:

> Into this Universe, and *Wh*y not knowing,
>
> Nor *Wh*ence, like *W*ater, *w*illy-nilly flowing,
>
> And out of it, as *W*ind along the *W*aste,
>
> I know not *Wh*ither, *w*illy-nilly blowing.
>
> FITZGERALD: *Rubaiyat of Omar Khayyam*

> And all should cry, *B*eware! *B*eware!
>
> His *fl*ashing eyes, his *fl*oating hair!
>
> COLERIDGE: *Kubla Khan*

> All the *b*lue *b*onnets are *b*ound for the *B*order.
>
> SCOTT

Push off, and sitting well in order smite
The sounding furrows; for my purpose holds
To sail beyond the sunset. . . .

TENNYSON: Ulysses

Or bid me die, and I will dare
E'en death to die for thee.

HERRICK: To Anthea

Here are some examples of the more subtle effect of crossed alliteration:

No longer mourn for me when I am dead
Than you shall hear the surly sullen bell
Give warning to the world that I am fled
From this vile world, with vilest worms to dwell:
Nay, if you read this line, remember not
The hand that writ it; for I love you so
That I in your sweet thoughts would be forgot
If thinking on me then should make you woe.[1]

SHAKESPEARE

In these lines it will be noticed that where there is strong, direct emphasis, as in the 'surly sullen bell', there is piled alliteration, but the pattern of alliteration becomes more complex as the thought becomes more subtle.

How soon hath Time, the subtle thief of youth,
Stol'n on his wing my three and twentieth year!

MILTON

has crossed alliteration on four different consonants. Here are a few more examples:

[1] *Wr*, of course, alliterates to *r*, and *th*inking does not alliterate with *th*en; we must always be guided by the ear, not the eye.

Time and *d*eath shall *d*epart and say in *f*lying
Love has *f*ound out a way to *li*ve by *d*ying.

DRYDEN

Come *S*leep; O *S*leep! the *c*ertain knot of *p*eace,
The *b*aiting-*p*lace of *w*it, the *b*alm of *w*oe,
The *p*oor man's *w*ealth, the *p*risoner's release. . . .

SIR PHILIP SIDNEY

*F*air eyes, who asks more *h*eat than comes from *h*ence,
*H*e in a *f*ever wishes pestilence.

DONNE

Give *li*fe to this *d*ark *w*orld *w*hich *li*eth *d*ead.

DRUMMOND of HAWTHORNDEN

While the Cock with lively *d*in
*S*catters the rear of *d*arkness thin
And to the *st*ack, or the *B*arn *d*ore,
*St*outly *st*ruts his *D*ames *b*efore.

MILTON: *L'Allegro*

Alliteration is by no means the only kind of repeated sound
in a poem other than rhyme. Let us look at a verse from John
Donne:

*W*hen *th*ou sigh'st, *th*ou *s*igh'st not *w*ind
But *s*igh'st my *s*oul away;
*W*hen thou *w*eep'st, unkindly kind,
My life's blood *d*oth *d*ecay.
It cannot be
*Th*at *th*ou lov'st me, as *th*ou *s*ay'st,
If in *th*ine my life *th*ou *w*aste,
*Th*at art the best of me.

First of all, there is an obvious pattern of alliteration; but there
is also a frequent repetition of the i-sound in 'sigh', 'kindly',

'thine', 'my', 'life' and (then) 'Wind'. This is a sound whose common emotional significance can be guessed from its appearance in such words as 'whining', 'pining', 'crying', 'sighing', 'decline'—a sound often suggesting sorrow and depression.[1] It is also a rather long vowel which slows the movement of the lines in their naturally rather rapid rhythm. The numerous -st sounds are dictated by grammatical necessity rather than art, but the repetition does help to build up emphasis, and contributes something to the effect of the s-alliteration.

In Milton's beautiful word-picture:

> . . . the high embowed roof,
> With antic pillars massy proof,
> And storied windows richly dight,
> Casting a dim religious light.
> There let the pealing organ blow
> To the full-voiced choir below,

alliteration, though it exists, is not dominant. There are several other kinds of sound-echo. As a bit of red ribbon at the throat of a dress may be 'caught up' by a red bracelet on the wrist, so 'pillars' and 'windows' catch up each other's sounds, and 'storied' and 'organs' do so even more, being words with the same stressed vowel followed by an unstressed vowel which has become neutral in its unstressed position. *Religious* has in the centre a link between the vowel of *dim* and the initial consonant of *light*, and 'light' and 'let' (in the next line) are perfect pararhymes. The l-sound keeps appearing in the middle of words. There are several other internal echoes that I am deliberately leaving for the intelligent reader to find.

[1] I am well aware that the vowel is also found in *dining* and *wining*; it is dangerous to generalize too *wildly*.

Perhaps in *The Raven* Edgar Allen Poe rather overdoes the use of internal rhymes, alliterations, echoes and resemblances of all kinds; but it will be instructive and perhaps interesting for the reader to work out all these in the final verse:

And the Raven, never flitting, still is sitting, still is sitting
On the pallid bust of Pallas, just above my chamber door;
And his eyes have all the seeming of a demon's that is
        dreaming,
And the lamplight o'er him streaming throws his shadow on
       the floor
And my soul from out that shadow that lies floating on the
        floor
Shall be lifted—nevermore!

Swinburne is another poet who uses a great many internal echoes:

  And the high gods took in hand
  Fire, and the falling of tears,
  And a measure of sliding sand
  From under the feet of the years;
  And froth and drift of the sea;
  And dust of the labouring earth;
  And bodies of things to be
  In the houses of death and birth;
  And wrought with weeping and laughter,
  And fashioned with loathing and love
  With life before and after
  And death beneath and above,
  For a day and a night and a morrow,
  That his strength might endure for a span
  With travail and heavy sorrow,
  The holy spirit of man.

Sometimes Swinburne uses this technique to excess, but he was witty enough to parody himself in *Nephelidia*:

From the depth of the dreamy decline of the dawn through a
    notable nimbus of nebulous moonshine,
Pallid and pink as the palm of the flag-flower that
     flickers with fear of the flies as they
      float,
Are the looks of our lovers that lustrously lean from a
    marvel of mystic miraculous moonshine,
These that we feel in the blood of our blushes that
     thicken and threaten with throbs through the
      throat? . . .

I have seen the term *melopoeia* (originally used for the making of melodies, especially for dramatic use) used for this excess of word-music, but not generally.

VIII. FORM IN INTONATION

'... so I had to put my foot down in a very firm tone of voice ...'
Heard in a school staff-room

I T is possible for a poem to have quite a definite pattern of
of intonation, a pattern made only when the poem is read
aloud, by the ups-and-downs of the voice. This pattern is
more at the mercy of the reader than any other, for, as is well
known, we can alter the meaning of a sentence entirely by
altering the intonation. A friend of mine tells me that she
knows a highly intelligent women who is so completely tone-
deaf as not to understand when a sentence is spoken ironically;
she has several times been much embarrassed as a result. If we
misunderstand the meaning of a poem we are likely to read it
with the wrong intonation, much as, in *A Midsummer Night's
Dream*, Peter Quince, reciting mechanically a Prologue he
does not understand, runs over all the stops and talks nonsense:

> Consider then we come but in despite.
> We do not come as minding to content you.
> Our true intent is. All for your delight
> We are not here. That you should here repent you,
> The actors are at hand. . . .

Poems in which the intonation-pattern is important for
making a pattern of sound as well as conveying the sense will
tend to be those written in an ironical temper and in a col-

69

loquial style. There is an exact parallel of intonation in these two verses by Sir John Suckling:

> Why so pale and wan, fond lover?
> Prithee, why so pale?
> Will, when looking well can't win her,
> Looking ill prevail?
> Prithee, why so pale?
>
> Why so dull and mute, young sinner?
> Prithee, why so mute?
> Will, when speaking well can't win her,
> Saying nothing do't?
> Prithee, why so mute?

This repetition leads us, as with a pattern of rhythm, to expect a third repetition of the pattern, and we receive an agreeable, amusing shock when the last verse has a very different intonation:

> Quit, quit for shame, this will not move;
> This cannot take her.
> If of herself she will not love,
> Nothing can make her;
> The devil take her!

The half-sympathetic, reasoning tone of the first two verses gives place to a robust and hearty dismissal of the whole matter.

Abraham Cowley, in his light-hearted poem *The Chronicle*, in which he relates a succession of love-fancies with great good humour, repeats a pattern of intonation in the middle of the poem, where he twice refers to one lady's conquest, moves in the fourth line into an explanation of how this queen

was deposed and in the final line discloses the name of the new
fancy:

> Another Mary then arose
> And did the rigorous laws impose;
> A mighty tyrant she!
> Long, alas, should I have been
> Under that iron-sceptred queen,
> Had not Rebecca set me free.
>
> When fair Rebecca set me free,
> 'Twas then a golden time with me.
> But soon these pleasures fled,
> For the gracious princess died
> In her youth and beauty's pride,
> And Judith reigned in her stead.

To read the whole of the poem is to see how, though he is
relating a catalogue, Cowley skilfully shifts the intonation
patterns so that no pattern becomes stereotyped, which would
make a poem of such length very dull.

There is a very close parallel of intonation in the last two
verses of Burns's *To the Unco Guid*; the parallel emphasizes the
move away from severe satire to gentle regret and charity; to
use one verse only would perhaps have made the poem seem
'top-heavy' or inconsistent in tone:

> Then gently scan your brother man,
> Still gentler sister woman;
> Thou they may gang a kennin wrang,
> To step aside is human;
> One point must still be greatly dark—
> The moving *Why* they do it;
> And just as lamely can ye mark

How far perhaps they rue it.

Who made the heart, 'tis He alone
Decidedly can try us;
He knows each chord, its various tone,
Each spring, its various bias;
Then at the balance let's be mute;
We never can adjust it;
What's done we partly may compute,
But know not what's resisted.

Edmund Waller's *On A Girdle* has in each verse two lines of statement followed by two more strongly emotional lines; the intonation for the three verses is probably much the same, with a somewhat louder voice for the last two lines:

That which her slender waist confined,
Shall now my joyful temples bind;
No monarch but would give his crown,
His arms might do what this has done.

It was my heaven's extremest sphere,
The pale which held that lovely deer.
My joy, my grief, my hope, my love,
Did all within this circle move!

A narrow compass! and yet there
Dwelt all that's good and all that's fair;
Give me but what this ribband bound,
Take all the rest the sun goes round.

Here, of course, the intonation is far from exactly symmetrical.

While it is interesting to look for parallels and patterns of intonation in a poem, it is more generally instructive to notice how wonderfully a great poet will avoid monotony, and how a good reciter follows the intention of the poet.

IX. THE USE OF REPETITION

(A) INTELLECTUAL EFFECT

A double blessing is a double grace.
SHAKESPEARE: *Hamlet*

WHENEVER we start discussing pattern in poetry, we are discussing repetition; rhythm, rhyme, alliteration and internal echoes are all repetitions of sounds; but the repetition of whole words or phrases is as much a part of the mental as of the physical form. We all know how repetition helps us to learn such things as the conjugation of a foreign verb or a list of dates, and how much advertising and propaganda depend on repetition to convince us of things that are often not true. All teachers soon find that they have to say something several times before every member of the class has absorbed it. We also tend to repeat ourselves when we are very angry, happy, or distressed, and those who have never acquired the art of conversation irritate us by repeating themselves far too much. The repetition of words is used for emphasis in all these situations. The repetition of a word or a phrase for the sake of this intellectual effect—to emphasize a fact or idea—is quite different from the function of repetition in a refrain or chorus; this will be treated in the next chapter.

Repetition of a single word is very common, as in speech;

it is used for emphasis, much as an Indian friend of mine used to describe a kitten as a 'small small cat'.

> A little buttery, and therein
> A little bin
> Which keeps my little loaf of bread
> Unchipp'd, unflead:
>
> HERRICK

> The mountains look on Marathon
> And Marathon looks on the sea.
>
> BYRON

> It is the cause, it is the cause, my soul!
> Let me not name it to you, you chaste stars!
> It is the cause.
>
> SHAKESPEARE

> Sleep, O sleep,
> With thy rod of incantation,
> Charm my imagination.
>
> GAY

> Fallen, fallen, fallen, fallen, fallen from his high
> estate.
>
> DRYDEN

A single word may also be repeated many times in order to work up to an emotional climax:

> Let him have time to tear his curled hair,
> Let him have time against himself to rave,
> Let him have time of Time's help to despair,
> Let him have time to live a loathed slave,
> Let him have time a beggar's orts to crave,
> And time to see one that by alms doth live
> Disdain to him disdained scraps to give.

74

Let him have time to see his friends his foes,
And merry fools to mock at him resort;
Let him have time to mark how slow time goes
In time of sorrow, and how swift and short
His time of folly, and his time of sport;
And ever let his unrecalling crime
Have time to wail the abusing of his time.

SHAKESPEARE: *The Rape of Lucrece*

How do I love thee? Let me count the ways.
I love thee to the depth and breadth and height
My soul can reach, when feeling out of sight
For the ends of Being and ideal Grace.
I love thee to the level of everyday's
Most quiet need, by sun and candlelight.
I love thee freely, as men strive for Right;
I love thee purely, as they turn from Praise.
I love thee with the passion put to use
In my own griefs, and with my childhood's faith.
I love thee with a love I seemed to lose
With my lost saints,—I love thee with the breath,
Smiles, tears, of all my life!—and, if God choose,
I shall but love thee better after death.

ELIZABETH BARRETT BROWNING

In the hands of a master this prolonged repetition can be thus magnificent. Obviously, in an inferior poet, who resembles not so much the brilliant artist as the bad talker, it can be very dull. The

Ay me, alas! ay me, alas! come, Time, take everything away,
For all is thine, be it good or bad that grows.

of the minor Elizabethan poet Thomas Proctor is not par-

75

ticularly impressive, nor is Tennyson's *Riflemen Form*; all
readers of poetry should bear in mind that, just as there are
many fine poems written by minor poets, sometimes single
poems by which alone a poet is known, there are many lapses
in the work of most of the major poets. We should never be
completely and slavishly uncritical.

The repetition of a phrase is as common as the repetition of
a word, and, like the repetition of a word, serves to give
emphasis:

> Tell arts they have no soundness,
> But vary by esteeming;
> Tell schools they want profoundness,
> And stand too much on seeming:
> If arts and schools reply,
> Give arts and schools the lie.
>
> SIR WALTER RALEIGH

> Dost thou laugh to see how fools are vexed
> To add to golden numbers, golden numbers?
>
> DEKKER

> In vain, in vain—the all-composing hour
> Resistless falls: the Muse obeys the Power.
> She comes! she comes! the sable throne behold
> Of Night primeval and of Chaos old!
>
> POPE: *The Dunciad*

> All we are against thee, against thee, O God most high.
>
> SWINBURNE

> I am! yet what I am who cares, or knows?
>
> JOHN CLARE

> Arm! Arm! it is—it is—the cannon's opening roar!
>
> BYRON: *Childe Harold's Pilgrimage*

Repetition, not of an exact phrase but of the structure of a phrase, is a very common device:

> Like the dew on the mountain,
> Like the foam on the river,
> Like the bubble on the fountain,
> Thou art gone, and for ever!
>
> SCOTT

> My heart is like a singing bird
> Whose nest is in a watered shoot;
> My heart is like an apple tree
> Whose boughs are bent with thickset fruit;
> My heart is like a rainbow shell
> That paddles in a halcyon sea;
> My heart is gladder than all these
> Because my love is come to me.
>
> CHRISTINA ROSSETTI

> No princely pomp, no wealthy store,
> No force to win the victory,
> No wily wit to salve a sore,
> No shape to feed a loving eye;
> To none of these I yield as thrall:
> For why? My mind doth serve for all.
>
> SIR EDWARD DYER

Or, to add a humorous verse:

> For one good wife Ulysses slew
> A worthy knot of gentle blood;
> For one ill wife Greece overthrew
> The town of Troy. Sith bad and good
> Bring mischief, Lord, let be Thy will
> To keep me free from either ill.
>
> ANONYMOUS (sixteenth century)

77

There are other and considerably more subtle devices of repetition. It is possible to play with a word, using it several times with a slightly different meaning each time:

> Diaphenia, like the spreading roses,
> That in thy sweet all sweets encloses,
> Fair sweet, how I do love thee!
> I do love thee as each flower
> Loves the sun's life-giving power;
> For dead, thy breath to life might move me.
>
> HENRY CONSTABLE

This is pretty but trivial; but how shatteringly startling, how daring, in the best sense, is the passionate and holy pun at the end of John Donne's *Hymn to God the Father*:[1]

> I have a sin of fear, that when I have spun
> My last thread, I shall perish on the shore;
> Swear by Thyself that at my death Thy Son
> Shall shine as he shines now and heretofore;
> And having done that Thou hast done,
> I fear no more.

The 'Son' is a 'sun' that shines as well as the Son of God; the final repetition of 'done' makes a symmetrical pattern with the other two verses of this lovely poem, but I feel sure that the poet is also saying 'Thou, God, hast Donne—in Thy keeping for ever'. Puns can evidently be sublime as well as vulgar.[2]

It is possible to repeat something with a slight change to improve the modulation:

[1] We know that the name Donne was pronounced to rhyme with *bun*.

[2] See also Chapter XIII.

> For the sword outwears the sheath,
> And the soul wears out the breast.
>
> BYRON

Or, when ideas are paralleled, the number of words used for each idea, or the number of syllables, may be varied so as to avoid monotony in the rhythm:

> The One remains, the many change and pass;
> Heaven's light for ever shines, Earth's shadows fly.
>
> SHELLEY: Adonais

> For he who lives more lives than one
> More deaths than one must die.
>
> OSCAR WILDE

Some slight reversal or modification of the normal word order may lend great weight to the words:

> Some little talk awhile of Me and Thee
> There was—and then no more of Thee and Me.
>
> Rubaiyat of Omar Khayyam

> Hierusalem, my happy home,
> When shall I come to thee?
> When shall my sorrows have an end?
> Thy joys when shall I see?
>
> ANONYMOUS (seventeenth century)

This kind of device needs to be used with discretion, or the poet will invert the word order so artificially that the result is unpleasant. Inversion is supposed to be a feature of 'poetic licence' and is freely used by beginners and bad poets who cannot otherwise push their rhyme words to the end of the lines, but good poets use it only (in their good poems) where it also gives some special emphasis. This is from a noble and very popular poem, but is it not somewhat dislocated?

> Oft did the harvest to their sickle yield,
> Their furrow oft the stubborn glebe has broke;
> How jocund did they drive their team afield!
> How bowed the woods beneath their sturdy stroke!
> GRAY: *Elegy Written in A Country Churchyard*

It is plain that here Gray is trying to repeat a general idea in four examples without monotony, but he has altered the word order so much as to upset the natural flow of the English language. He was writing in a period of much artificiality; but it may also be helpful to remember that Gray, like many of the most artificial of English poets, had a classical education, and was accustomed to the literatures of Latin and Greek, in which word-order obeys different rules and has more to do with emphasis.

The last type of repetition for its intellectual effect is the repetition of the whole structure of a verse, with only a few words changed; to demonstrate this I must quote a whole poem:

> O she looked out of the window,
> As white as any milk;
> But he looked into the window
> As black as any silk.
>
> Hulloa, hulloa, hulloa, hulloa you coal black smith!
> O what is your silly song?
> You never shall change my maiden name
> That I have kept so long;

I'd rather die a maid, yes, but then she said,
And be buried all in my grave,
Than I'd have such a nasty, husky, dusky, musty, fusky
     coal black smith;
A maiden I will die.

Then she became a duck,
A duck upon the stream;
And he became a water-dog,
And fetched her back again.
Hulloa, etc.

Then she became a hare,
A hare all on the plain;
And he became a greyhound dog
And fetched her back again.
Hulloa, etc.

Then she became a fly,
A fly all in the air;
And he became a spider,
And fetched her to his lair.
Hulloa, etc.[1]

This form in which the main structure remains the same is a
favourite of folk-song and other traditional songs that have
developed in communities and been composed by groups
rather than individuals. I do not doubt that practically every

---

[1] There are several versions of this song and many more of the
general story. I am indebted for this version to Auden and Garrett:
The Poet's Tongue.

residential college, school or barracks in the country still composes such songs. This rather primitive use of repetition is really an admission of technical difficulties, but the effect is not unpleasant.

X. THE USE OF REPETITION

(B) PURE MAGICAL EFFECT

Thrice toss these oaken ashes in the air,
Thrice sit thou mute in this enchanted chair,
Then thrice three times tie up this true-love's knot,
And murmur soft, 'She will or she will not'.

THOMAS CAMPION

MAGIC makes great use of repetitions; we are all familiar with stories in which something has to be done or said three or seven times; religious rituals, which are more or less akin to primitive magic, depending on the degree of intellectual development, make great use of repetition with prayers for the various occasions of life, prayer-wheels, rosaries and repeated observances; and repetition plays a great part in the more primitive, emotional parts of our lives. We find that we can be greatly reassured by someone else repeating our own name in a tender and friendly manner, seriously demoralized by someone repeating it in hostile or sarcastic tones. Most teachers find that in learning the names of a new class they gain power over it. By repeating a word we seem to gain a sense of power over it, many dull talkers repeat what they think is a good phrase; children repeat new words they have learned with a persistence often wearying to adults, and older people often take the first opportunity to use a word they have just learned. The habit of swearing, especially when it becomes a habit divorced from emphasis, may have some such primitive significance; most of the English swear-words have meanings connected with religion, blood, or fertility, three of the very primitive human interests. When we study poetry intellectually, we must think of its effect on us and try to account for it; but we should not forget that if the poem is a good one the poet probably wrote it under the stimulus of some overwhelmingly powerful emotional urge, and some of the poet's emotion may be passed on to us by processes that are not conscious. Poetry is more akin to magic, prayer, prophecy and myth than to knitting or fretwork; to look at it purely from the formally technical point of view and never surrender to it is as misleading as to wallow all the time in indefinable emotion about it.

The relationship of poetry to religious ritual has sometimes been very close indeed in England. I am not myself strongly susceptible to ritual, being one of those awkward, necessary people who are inclined to suspect that whatever a dogmatic Authority says is sure to be wrong or Authority would not insist on our accepting it without question; but I think part of the immense pathos and emotional power of religious ritual and liturgy lies precisely in its *lack* of originality. The poignancy of the formulae of a funeral service is that they have been said many times over other bodies, in the presence of other mourners, and are thus loaded with the whole problem of human anguish at the inevitability of death. The Marriage Service of the Church of England is profoundly moving largely because the terrible vows have been made before so many times, are, in a sense, quite impossible of fulfilment and represent only the best aspirations of imperfect beings crystallized into a formula; these words are loaded with a million memories of effort and failure, hope and happiness and sorrow.

An example of this close relationship of ritual and poetry is to be found in the beautiful and terrifying *Lyke-Wake Dirge*.[1] It consists of a summary of what the dead are to expect in their journey towards heaven: Purgatory fire, the Brig'O'Dread, Whinny-muir[2] and the consequences of their own evil actions or the relief brought by their good actions. This is intellectual enough; indeed, in its simple justice it is almost mathematical:

> If ever thou gavest hosen and shoon,
> Sit thee down and put them on;
>
> If hosen and shoon thou ne'er gavest none,
> The whinnies shall prick thee to the bare bone. . . .

but, like a pulse beat under the summary of the facts, runs a double refrain. Let us look at the first verse with its refrain:

> This ae night, this ae night,
> *Every night and all,*
> Fire and fleet and candle-light,
> *And Christ receive thy saule.*

The use of 'Every night and all' adds nothing to the intellectual meaning of the poem; to say it once would theoretically be sufficient; but the repetition heightens the emotional effect of its real, implied meaning, which is something like this: 'This watch by the dead has to take place every night; people die every day; you too must die, perhaps sooner than you think; every night brings its own peril of death.' More important, 'And Christ receive thy saule' is the proper, tradi-

---

[1] Benjamin Britten has made it even more terrifying by a remarkable musical setting.

[2] Thorny Moor.

tional thing to say; it is helpful to the fleeting soul, yet by its finality it is also terrifying. (A modern reader may be reminded of the inexorable sound of 'May the Lord have mercy on your soul' when a person is condemned to death. It is undoubtedly meant to be helpful, but must be terrifying to hear.) There is the further implication: 'Soon we shall say this formula again—for you.'

Many old ballads have a refrain which appears to be nearly meaningless but carries very heavy implications. There is a well-known ballad, generally called *The Cruel Mother*, telling of a woman who murders her twin babies to save herself from disgrace, and is later haunted by their ghosts and tortured by remorse. This horrible theme has for its double refrain 'Fine flowers in the valley' and 'And the green leaves they grow rarely'. These lines seem almost frivolously pretty in such a context, but in fact they serve to emphasize the grim theme by contrast, as a white background emphasizes a black object. Spring, the time for gay and reckless love, the flower of the valley (not the austere loneliness of the mountain heights), love so often compared to a flower for its beauty or its transience, which also causes the shameful fruit of unwise love; delight in the miracle of Spring that always withers—these are the suggestions; the ballad ends with an additional refrain line which is horrifyingly ironical in its context of eternal torment:

> But now we're in the heavens hie,
> Fine flowers in the valley—
> And ye have the pains of hell to drie,
> And the green leaves they grow rarely.
> Ten thousand times good-night and be wi' thee.

This is rather like the madness of Ophelia, increasing the sense of horror by allusions to pretty things.

86

Dunbar in his famous *Lament for the Makaris* (poets) uses as his refrain *Timor mortis conturbat me* (The fear of death disturbs me). Latin as an ornament to Scots verse may seem a little incongruous, perhaps even affected; it was not unusual in Dunbar's day, but it is also very impressive by its associations. Latin is the language of Catholic ritual, and the suggestion of a burial service heightens the sense both of fear and of the inevitability of death—the common human situation for which the formulae are provided. There may be a further implication: 'I use a Latin tag, therefore I am an educated man, a "clerk" not a "lewd man", and I can speak authoritatively about the death of poets.'

Not all refrains, however, are so obvious in their function, so, as we may put it, obviously sensible. *Binnorie*, a favourite ballad, has as its refrains: 'Binnorie, O Binnorie!' and 'By the bonny mill-dams o' Binnorie' which, while appropriate enough to some of the verses, are absurdly inappropriate to others. The ballad of *Earl Brand* has as its refrains the meaningless 'Ay lally, O lilly lally', curiously light and gay for the grim theme, and 'All in the night so early', which is not appropriate to the whole poem. Little sense can be extracted from the refrain 'As the dow (dove) flies over the mulberry tree' in *The Riddling Knight*, 'With a hey lillelu and a how lo lan' and 'And the birk and the broom blows bonnie' in *Hynd Horn*, or 'Eh, wow, bonnie!' in *Babylon*, in which the story is anything but 'bonnie'! The early ballads are the best-known English poems with refrains, though many, including some of the greatest, have none. Some of the early carols, in the wide sense of the word, which does not confine them to Christmas carols,[1] have refrains that sound more like exer-

[1] The interested reader should try to find in a library the monumental and fascinating *Early English Carols* by Greene.

cises for the correction of faulty speech than poetry. Some of these may have existed mainly to help people to keep time in the dance which was an accompaniment of primitive song. Here is a remarkably meaningless refrain from a Furry Day Carol:[1]

> With Holan-to, sing merry, O,
> With Holan-to, sing merry,
> With Holan-to, sing merry, O,
> With Holan-to, sing merry!

To a modern ear this is merely irritating, perhaps embarrassing, though no doubt when it is sung, as it is obviously meant to be, it can sound delightful. It is notorious that the translated libretti of operas are often fatuous, but the audience enjoys the music and takes no notice of the words. The meaningless and silly refrain survives in commercial 'popular' songs, where music helps to carry it; but the 'popular' song is generally very debased literature and the ballad is not. The ballads include some of the finest short stories ever written.

The meaningless refrain is embarrassing to the self-conscious and easily-bored modern reader, and is extremely difficult to use in recitation, unless it is so onomatopoeic that it can be used frankly as a sound effect, as in *Old MacDougall Had a Farm*, sea shanties with a hauling movement, the railway song *Chickhanka*, or some of Vachel Lindsay. If such refrains have to be spoken they are generally more suitable for choral speech than for individual recitation; most primitive poetry seems to have been collective rather than personal. When the ballads were first recited the audience very likely joined in the

---

[1] Furry Day—Flowery Day, referring to May Day.

chorus, perhaps with some accompaniment such as clapping or stamping.[1] The divorce between good poetry and music is a relatively modern phenomenon; most sixteenth-century lyrics were intended to be sung; and there are signs to-day of an attempt to bring them together again. If poetry and music could once more be brought into double harness in something more worthwhile than commercial 'plugged' popular songs and musical comedy, refrains and meaningless words might cease to be embarrassing and resume their function of ritual and suggestion.[2]

One of the functions of a ritual-like refrain is that of some aspects of religious ritual, also used less worthily by totalitarian politicians, a kind of hypnotic conditioning of the mind in which we are less critical of what is being said to us. A meaningless noise, if pleasant, has a soothing effect and repetition is reassuring. The refrain, like drum-beats in primitive ritual, may help to bring the audience into a receptive mood.

In examining poetry which has a meaningless refrain, however, the reader should bear in mind the possibility that the refrain may be, not a meaningless formula, but a group of words that have lost their meaning merely in the course of time. The reader who sees in the very old Shetland ballad *Sir Orfeo* 'Scowan ürla grün' and 'Whar giortan han grün orlac' as refrains may be forgiven for calling them gibberish, but in fact the difficulty is only linguistic; the lines mean 'Early green's the wood' and 'Where the hart goes yearly'. The rest

---

[1] All statements about folk art need to be taken with a spoonful of salt; there are many different theories.

[2] Examples of modern correlation of poetry and music are Britten's *Serenade for Tenor, Horn and Strings*, using poems of other periods, and William Walton's settings for Edith Sitwell's *Façade*, an example of *contemporary* poetry interpreted by a contemporary composer.

of the ballad has developed into recognizable English but the refrain has remained in early Shetland dialect.

Some refrains, as in some nursery rhymes, contain topical allusions which are now lost; it has been suggested that this is so in, for example, 'Georgie-Porgie Puddin'-an-Pie'. A nursery-school inspector once told me a rather horrifying example of topical allusions up to date in nursery rhyme; nursery school children playing a favourite game were heard to sing happily:

> Ring-a-ring-o'-roses,
> Pocket-ful of posies;
> Hiroshima,
> We all fall down!

The children were probably (one hopes so!) quite unconscious that they were helping to strengthen a comtemporary myth.

The idea that refrains have a ritual rather than an artistic force is supported by the fact that, whereas some of the old ballads and carols are unforgettable and are widely acclaimed as masterpieces of largely unconsious art, the use of the refrain by later writers, often themselves masters of their art has tended to fall flat. Tennyson's *Mariana* is perhaps one of the most successful of modern poems with a refrain; it is musical, delicate and full of Tennyson's characteristically vivid pictures of sight and sound; but, melodious as it is, the refrain:

> She only said, 'The night is dreary,
> He cometh not,' she said;
> She said, 'I am aweary, aweary,
> I would that I were dead!'

palls somewhat before the end of the poem. Henry Duff Traill, a rather unkind but witty parodist of the end of the

nineteenth century, irritated by the use of the refrain in poems
by the Rossettis and William Morris, ends one parody:

> Awakeneth
> Slowly, but sure awakening it has,
> The common sense of man; and I, also!
> The ballad-burden trick, now known too well,
> Am turned to scorn, and grown contemptible—
> A too transparent artifice to pass.
> What a cheap dodge I am! The cats who dart
> Tin-kettled through the streets in wild surprise
> Assail judicious ears not otherwise;
> And yet no critics praise the urchin's 'art',
> Who to the wretched creature's caudal part
> Its foolish empty-jingling 'burden' ties.[1]

The refrain is now almost entirely abandoned except in
humorous verse, though it survives in the folk-poetry of
pockets of unsophisticated peasantry and in such modern folk
art as the coarse songs of soldiers.

One type of refrain, less primitive, remains to be mentioned; it is not common, but can be impressive; it is that in
which the refrain changes slightly for each verse, though
keeping some repetition. This is perhaps more satisfying to
the modern mind, because it is more logical and also gives us
a small agreeable surprise each time. A great example of this is
Spenser's *Epithalamion*, in which the last line of the first verse
is:

> The woods shall to me answer and my echo ring.

[1] The complete parody may be found in Sir John Squire's delightful
anthology of parodies, *Apes and Parrots* (Herbert Jenkins, 1928). Many
of these parodies are very stimulating to thought about poetic technique.

A modified form of this line ends every verse, but it is not a simple repetitive refrain; it is connected with the sense of the previous line or lines. It seems rather cruel to cut off the tails of the twenty-three verses for a demonstration, but this will make the art clear; the reader will, I hope, look up the whole poem as soon as possible:

verse 2. And whilst she doth her dight,
    Do ye to her of joy and solace sing,
    That all the woods may answer and your echo ring.

verse 3. For she will waken straight,
    The whiles do ye this song unto her sing;
    The woods shall to you answer and your echo ring.

verse 4. Be also present here,
    To help to deck her and to help to sing,
    That all the woods may answer and your echo ring.

verse 5. For they of joy and pleasance to you sing,
    That all the woods may answer and your echo ring.

verse 6. And as ye use to Venus, to her sing,
    The whiles the woods shall answer and your echo ring.

verse 7. Then I thy sovereign praises loud will sing,
    That all the woods shall answer and their echo ring.

verse 8. And evermore they Hymen, Hymen, sing,
    That all the woods them answer and their echo ring.

verse 9. Nathless do ye still loud her praises sing,
    That all the woods may answer and your echo ring.

verse 10. Whiles ye forget your former lay to sing,
    To which the woods did answer and your echo ring?

verse 11. Then would ye wonder and her praises sing,
   That all the woods should answer and your echo ring.

verse 12. The choristers the joyous anthem sing,
   That all the woods may answer and their echo ring.

verse 13. Sing, ye sweet angels, Alleluia sing,
   That all the woods may answer and your echo ring.

verse 14. The whiles the maidens do their carol sing,
   To which the woods shall answer and their echo ring.

verse 15. And dance about them, and about them sing,
   That all the woods may answer, and your echo ring.

verse 16. As joying in the sight
   Of these glad many which for joy do sing,
   That all the woods them answer and their echo ring.

So far we have had a description of the wedding morning and the ceremony; at this point the couple are left alone together, the noises cease and the whole tone of the refrain changes.

verse 17. Now it is night, ye damsels may be gone,
   And leave my love alone,
   And leave likewise my former lay to sing;
   The woods no more shall answer, nor your echo ring.

verse 18. And let the maids and young men cease to sing;
   Ne let the woods them answer, nor their echo ring.

verse 19. Let none of these with dreary accents sing;
   Ne let the woods them answer, nor their echo ring.

verse 20. Now none doth hinder you, that say or sing;
   Ne will the woods now answer, nor your echo ring.

verse 21. Till which we cease our hopeful hap to sing;
      Ne let the woods us answer, nor our echo ring.

verse 22. Till which we cease your further praise to sing;
      Ne any woods shall answer, nor your echo ring.

verse 23. And cease till then our timely joys to sing;
      The woods no more shall answer, nor our echo ring.

By this rather irreverent process I have tried to show how in such a highly sophisticated and conscious work of art the refrain is an integral part of each verse. The student will find it interesting to compare the refrain in Spenser's *Prothalamion*. Another and more complicated 'modified refrain' is to be found in Sir Walter Raleigh's *The Lie*. The general theme of this brave but bitter poem is that the poet is dying and his soul must go out and give the lie to all human activities. It is a strong, insolent, sincere poem, epigrammatic in style. The first verse runs:

> Go, soul, the body's guest,
> Upon a thankless arrant;
> Fear not to touch the best;
> The truth shall be thy warrant.
> Go, since I needs must die,
> And give the world the lie.

As the poet goes on to describe the various falsities of the world in detail, the last line fluctuates appropriately:

> If church and court reply,
> Then give them both the lie.

> If potentates reply,
> Give potentates the lie.

And if they once reply
Then give them all the lie.

And if they make reply,
Then give them all the lie.

And wish them not reply,
For thou must give the lie.

And as they shall reply,
Give every one the lie.

And when they do reply,
Straight give them both the lie.

And as they do reply,
So give them still the lie.

And if they will reply,
Then give them all the lie.

If arts and schools reply,
Give arts and schools the lie.

And if they do reply,
Spare not to give the lie.

After using this uncompromising varied refrain through the poem, Raleigh drops it in the last verse, thus giving the reader a shock that reinforces the impact of the noble arrogance of his bitterness:

So when thou hast, as I
Commanded thee, done blabbing,
Although to give the lie
Deserves no less than stabbing,
Stab at thee he that will,
No stab the soul can kill.

Sometimes a poem can look as if it is going to have a regular refrain, but abandon regularity in favour of interest. This chapter may well conclude with a brief and very lovely example:

Never weather-beaten sail more willing bent to shore,
Never tired pilgrim's limbs affected slumber more,
Than my weary spright now longs to fly out of my troubled
    breast.
O! come quickly, sweetest Lord, and take my soul to rest.

Ever blooming are the joys of Heaven's high Paradise.
Cold age there deafs not our ears, nor vapour dims our eyes.
Glory there the sun outshines, whose beams the blessed only
    see.
O! come quickly, glorious Lord, and raise my spright to thee.

CAMPION

XI. MENTAL FORM

THE MAIN TYPES OF POETRY

Ay, in the catalogue ye go for men;
As hounds, and greyhounds, mongrels, spaniels, curs,
Shoughs, water-rugs, and demi-wolves, are clept
All by the name of dogs; the valued file
Distinguishes the swift, the slow, the subtle . . .

SHAKESPEARE: *Macbeth*

REPETITIVE patterns of words, which imply ideas, are more intellectual than patterns of sounds. We have devoted ten chapters mainly to the physical form of a poem, and must now come to the mental form, a more advanced study and one which cannot be learned mechanically. Someone who is quite indifferent to poetry can make, in an examination, a reasonably correct mark-earning analysis of the physical form of a poem; real appreciation, however, depends on the power to grasp the content of the poem and, as it were, to fuse appreciation of the content with consciousness of the form. A full study of the mental form of poetry would demand a book as big as the *Shorter Oxford English Dictionary*, whose title always amuses my students. Indeed, no comprehensive book will ever be written on the subject; there is too much to be said. The next few chapters will try merely to suggest a few directions, to be not a map, but a compass;

the compass will no doubt suffer a few magnetic variations whenever it comes near anything electrical in my personality.

The importance of the meaning of a poem can be over-rated. We all know the irritating person, usually middle-aged, who examines a modern poem and says he cannot understand it. He may not be meant to understand it intellectually, but to subject himself to the effect of a group of associations, to listen to an agreeable noise or even to suffer an erudite practical joke. However, the majority of poems have meaning that can in part be discussed intellectually, though with some inevitable loss of richness.[1]

A poem may, in content, be anything from a very short and simple expression of a single mood:

> Lay a garland on my hearse
> Of the dismal yew;
> Maidens, willow branches bear;
> Say, I died true.
>
> My love was false, but I was firm
> From the hour of birth.
> Upon my buried body lie
> Lightly, gentle earth!
>
> JOHN FLETCHER

to something as large and complex as *Paradise Lost*. For a long time poetry has been divided into various main types such as epic, lyric, dramatic or narrative. I will try to give a brief account of the types of intellectual structure in poetry, in descending order of size. The reader should resist the temptation to think that either largeness or smallness is a proof of

---

[1] I use 'intellectual' to denote what can be reasoned about and defined in words. There are many other mental processes.

merit, and should also remember that, as with everything that has life, types cannot usually be very sharply defined; there will be possible subdivisions, exceptions, overlaps and inter-mediate types.

EPIC

is the longest kind of poem. It tells a story, generally a well-known one and always one of heroic action. The action is not trivial. There is generally a good deal of physical or spiritual conflict, or both. Some of the characters are portrayed in great detail. The style is very dignified, generally rather ornate and formal; the figures of speech used are often very elaborate. The epic, a form found relatively early in the history of any literature, is often prompted in part by nationalist feeling. Its verse form is often, though not invariably, relatively simple. The epics from which most examples have been drawn in critical theory are Homer's *Iliad* and *Odyssey* and Virgil's *Aeneid*

Examples: Milton, *Paradise Lost*, *Paradise Regained*; Spenser, *The Faerie Queene*; Giles Fletcher, *Christ's Victory*; Blake, *Milton*.

EPIC NARRATIVE

I would use this term to denote poems in the dignified, formal style associated with epic, or in some other highly ornamented style, telling a story of heroic action or suffering, but with one simple action and without the length and complexity of the true epic. Anyone who says: 'How long is an epic?' is asking a question rather like: 'How long is a piece of string?' but per-haps a convenient distinction may be that an Epic Narrative can be read at one sitting and an Epic is not normally read all at once.

Examples: Chaucer, *The Prioresses Tale*, *The Clerk's Tale*; Shakespeare, *Venus and Adonis*, *The Rape of Lucrece*; Sackville,

Induction to the Mirror for Magistrates; Tennyson, *The Idylls of the King* (several narratives); Matthew Arnold, *Sohrab and Rustum*; John Masefield, *The Everlasting Mercy, Dauber*; C. Day Lewis, *Nabara*.

SIMPLE NARRATIVE

This term may be used for a 'round, unvarnished tale', in which the style is simple and direct and the story all-important. The thrill of this is due generally to the very simplicity and directness of the style.

Examples: All the old ballads; Cowper, *John Gilpin*; Coleridge, *Rime of the Ancient Mariner*; A. E. Housman, *Hell Gate*; Wordsworth, *Michael, The Idiot Boy*.

VERSE ESSAY

A piece of thoughtful verse on some topic of interest, neither a story nor an expression of personal emotion. This may be of two kinds: a *didactic* verse essay giving good advice or information or discussing something in a calm way.

Examples: Sir John Davies, *Nosce Teipsum, Orchestra*; George Herbert, *The Church Porch*; Louis MacNeice, *Autumn Journal*.

A *satire*, which will contain much that is didactic, but is also intended to arouse laughter by its witty and severe criticism of abuses.

Examples: Pope, *The Dunciad*; Byron, *English Bards and Scotch Reviewers, Hints from Horace, The Age of Bronze*; Dryden, *Absalom and Achitophel*; Roy Campbell, *The Wayzgoose, The Georgiad*.

ODE

is nowadays used to classify a fairly long and stately poem written on some public occasion or addressed to some person, thing or personified quality.

Examples: Dryden, *Ode for Saint Cecilia's Day*; Keats, *Ode to a Nightingale, Ode on a Grecian Urn*; Shelley, *Ode to the West Wind, Hymn to Intellectual Beauty*; Wordsworth, *Ode to Duty*; Tennyson, *Ode on the Death of the Duke of Wellington*; C. Day Lewis, *Ode to Fear*.

LYRIC

A fairly short poem expressing emotion. Originally it always meant a poem intended to be sung, and has kept something of this meaning. The early definition is embarrassing, as some people can sing almost anything and some cannot sing at all, so we can hardly test a lyric by trying to sing it. A lyric is, however, to be thought of as being fairly simple and musical in diction. Most short poems may be classed as lyrics. The Sonnet is lyrical in subject though perhaps not in form. The Elizabethan madrigal is a true lyric in every sense. A subdivision of lyric is the *Elegy*, a poem, long or short, of mourning or on some sorrowful theme. To give examples of lyric is unnecessary; the student should read Palgrave's *Golden Treasury of Songs and Lyrics* if examples are required.

EPIGRAM

is a very short poem, usually two, four or six lines, crisply and concisely written, with a stinging climax; its function is to display wit.

Examples:

> His whole life is an epigram, smart, smooth,
>   and neatly penned,
> Plaited quite neat to catch applause, with
>   a hang-noose at the end.

BLAKE

'Tis done; I yield; adieu, thou cruel fair!
Adieu, the averted face, the ungracious
    check!
I go to die, to finish all my care,
'To hang.'—'To hang?'—'Yes, round another's
    neck.'

LEIGH HUNT

Here lies my wife! here let her lie!
Now she's at rest, and so am I.

DRYDEN

Various kinds of poem distinguished by their physical form
will be discussed in Chapter XV.

All the types of poem mentioned above are such as can
logically be read by a single voice, provided that neither the
reader nor the audience becomes physically weary. There is,
however, a large body of magnificent poetry requiring more
than one voice for correct interpretation, namely, dramatic
poetry and certain subdivisions of this. Dramatic poetry includes the plays of Shakespeare, Marlowe, Webster, Beau-
mont and Fletcher, Tourneur, Middleton, Dekker, Ford,
Marston, Jonson (some), Byron, Shelley, T. S. Eliot, Louis
MacNeice and Christopher Fry, as well as Milton's *Samson
Agonistes* and other plays based on classical models. Some
dramatic poetry, such as the plays of Shakespeare, Webster or
Eliot, is intended for the stage and highly suitable to it. Other
plays in verse, though having dramatic form, are more suited
to reading in silence; the plays of Byron and Shelley probably
come into this category. A verse-play, like any other play, may
be full length or one act, in a historical, fantastic or contemporary setting, in modern, archaic or stylized diction. It is not
wise to look at the poetry in a dramatic poem simply as

poetry and with no regard for its dramatic function; the latter may serve to explain some apparent flatness or crudity, some far-fetched image or ugly sound, as appropriate to the character or situation.

There is also what might be called semi-dramatic poetry, in which more than one person is speaking, but stage production is not intended. Examples of this not very common form are *The Nutbrown Maid* (anonymous); Daniel, *Poet and Critic, Ulysses and the Siren*; Browning, *In a Gondola, In a Balcony*; Louis MacNeice, *An Eclogue for Christmas, Eclogue by a Five-barred Gate*. The purpose of such an untheatrical dialogue is generally to clarify a contrast of ideas, ideals or characters.

Lastly, there is the dramatic lyric, in which the poet speaks with a single voice that is not his own. He is trying to give sympathetic, explanatory expression to an alien personality.

Examples: Browning, *My Last Duchess, Caliban upon Setebos, The Bishop Orders his Tomb*; Tennyson, *Tithonus, St. Simeon Stylites*; Yeats, *A Last Confession*; John Heath-Stubbs, *Stone-Age Woman*.

Such categories as these are useful in discussion; we need a critical vocabulary; but the student should beware of over-valuing a list of critical terms. They can be used wrongly, without intelligence or without qualification; worse, they can be used patronizingly. They are not magic passwords to open the door into the kingdom of poetry. The person who uses a wealth of critical jargon without thinking probably has less real appreciation of poetry than the person who hears a few lines never heard before and is haunted by them all day.

XII. MENTAL FORM

LOGICAL SEQUENCE

'Is, to dispute well, Logic's chiefest end?'
MARLOWE: *Dr. Faustus*

LOGIC, or the process of correct and disciplined reasoning, is a process entirely of the conscious mind and under our conscious control; it is, if anything, rather opposed to emotion. There is a certain level of experience at which we have what feels like an intellectual emotion; it is a condition in which we cannot often hope to be; I suspect it is the condition in which great poetry is written and I know it is to be found in human love, but it defies description. In ordinary human activity, the antithesis of reason and emotion is not questioned, and, though it may be one of the impossible tasks of the poet to reconcile the two, we can to some extent consider the two separately when discussing poetry.

A narrative poem has as its principal content the story, and a long poem of didactic or satirical intent has a plan that can be worked out much as we work out a plan before writing an essay, or ought to, unless we are geniuses. For instance, if we study Pope's *Essay on Criticism* we shall find that the plan is something like this:

1. The importance of sound critical standards:

   (a) Good natural taste rare.

(*b*)   But taste can be cultivated.

(*c*)   Description of bad and good critics.

2. Follow Nature; the rules are only 'Nature methodiz'd'. Study the classics for examples.

3. Pride is the chief cause of wrong judgments:

(*a*)   'A little learning is a dangerous thing.'

(*b*)   We should consider every work of art as a whole.

(*c*)   We cannot expect perfection.

(*d*)   We should not give all our attention to one aspect of the work of art, as (i) Imagery, (ii) Style, (iii) Rhythm.

(*e*)   It is best to avoid extremes.

(*f*)   Avoid copying the judgment of others in a servile way.

4. A passage of sympathy for the modern poet and of dispraise for obscenity.

5. A summary of the qualities of a good critic and a bad one.

6. A brief history of Criticism.

Obviously a prose essay of some merit and utility could have been written on the same plan. The difficulty in grasping the logical sequence is more often felt when dealing with a lyric or other short poem of mood or description. A lyric or other short poem usually has logical structure as one of its components. It need not; this nursery rhyme is hauntingly pretty, but has remarkably little sense:

> I had a little nut-tree, nothing would it bear
> But a silver nutmeg and a golden pear;
> The King of Spain's daughter came to visit me,
> And all was because of my little nut-tree.
> I skipped over water, I danced over sea,
> And all the birds in the air couldn't catch me,

Longer poems may also be difficult of interpretation. For instance, Blake's *Jerusalem*[1] is not a poem whose meaning leaps to the eye at the first reading; here is a brief extract:

Thus sang the Daughters in lamentation, uniting into One.
With Rahab as she turn'd the iron Spindle of destruction.
Terrified at the Sons of Albion they took the Falshood which
Gwendolen hid in her left hand; it grew and grew till it
Became a space and an Allegory around the winding Worm.
They named it Canaan and built for it a tender Moon.

The Surrealist artists in both words and pictures depend for their justification on the fact that most of our experiences are not logical and that our thoughts include all kinds of apparently absurd but sometimes very meaningful juxtapositions.

If we do not understand the meaning of a poem after several sympathetic readings, we should consider these possibilities in, I think, this order:

1. Should we perhaps be able to understand it if we knew some fact we do not at present know?

For example, some of Chaucer, Shakespeare and Milton is unintelligible without a slight knowledge of medieval astronomy and astrology. Some of Wordsworth is puzzling to one who has no idea of the theories of William Godwin. Nearly all English poets have some allusions to the figures of classical mythology. Many contemporary poets cannot be fully understood without some knowledge of Freud (Auden, MacNeice), Marxism (Day Lewis, Auden, Spender, Cornford, Caudwell), history and legend (Edith Sitwell), Jung and Blake (Kathleen

---

[1] The long poem of that title, not the lovely lyric, 'And did those feet in ancient time?' also called 'Blake's Jerusalem'.

Raine), Welsh myth and history (Vernon Watkins, Henry Treece), and so on. A poet can hardly expect everyone to grasp an allusion to, say, rhinolalia aperta or Ganesha, but it is reasonable for the poet to expect readers to be fairly familiar with the more important aspects of contemporary know-ledge, or at least to be able to understand a footnote. Ezra Pound and T. S. Eliot sometimes assume too much; their public will always be somewhat small; but the student should always remember that it is difficult to leave something out of our writing or conversation that is very much a part of our own mental equipment, even when we know that it is by no means common knowledge.

2. Is the poem an allegory or arrangement of symbols that we have missed?

> Having been tenant long to a rich Lord,
> Not thriving, I resolved to be bold,
> And make a suit unto him, to afford
> A new small-rented lease, and cancell th'old.
>
> In heaven at his manour I him sought;
> They told me there, that he was lately gone
> About some land, which he had dearly bought
> Long since on earth, to take possession.
>
> I straight return'd, and knowing his great birth,
> Sought him accordingly in great resorts;
> In cities, theatres, gardens, parks and courts:
> At length I heard a ragged noise and mirth
>
> Of theeves and murderers: there I him espied,
> Who straight, *Your suit is granted*, said, and died.
>
> GEORGE HERBERT

This, at first sight, seems a somewhat puzzling poem. The first verse makes perfectly good sense as a statement of someone's business arrangements, but what is 'heaven' doing in the next verse? And why is the rich Lord to be found among thieves and murderers? Has he been murdered? We might suspect a piece of social criticism; all rich lords are thieves and murderers in the sense in which 'property is theft' if they injure their fellow-men; but this lord, so far from being a tyrannical rich man, is kind and grants the tenant's suit even when he is dying and might be pardoned for not thinking about such a matter as someone else's lease. No, this will not do. The reader might be tempted to protest that 'This is not clear; it is not consistent.' I have deliberately cheated the reader by suppressing the title, which is *Redemption*. When we see that the poem is an allegory of the Fall of Man and the death of Christ after His Incarnation, the poem not only makes excellent sense but is very poignant. The intelligent student will be able to work out the details.

Many of the poems of Blake and certain contemporaries cannot be appreciated unless we look for this kind of half-hidden meaning.

3. Is the poem not intended to be 'understood'? That is, is it intended to have an effect on us entirely through our senses and the use of associations and not by a process of coherent thought? If so, we waste time and spoil the poem by hunting for intellectual meaning.

4. Lastly, and *after every other resort has been tried*, we are entitled to ask: Is this simply a bad poem, a poem that is not to be understood because it is badly written? Such a thing is possible even in the minor works of the great. There are even a few passages of Shakespeare that, as they stand, mean nothing. However, in any work that the ordinary non-special-

ist student is likely to meet there are far fewer bad or meaningless poems than the hasty or ignorant reader may be tempted
to think.

In a short poem that has, as most have, obvious coherent
meaning, there are three main kinds of structure, though of
course we could go on working out exceptions and subdivisions for another twenty pages. There is the kind in which the
poet simply leads up to a climax or summary, the poem in
which he turns round on himself with a contradiction and
that in which there is what might be called a dialectical
development. George Herbert in *Discipline* has such unity in
his treatment of the theme of the weakness of Man and the
power of God that he nearly repeats the first verse at the end:

> Throw away Thy rod,
> Throw away Thy wrath.
> O my God,
> Take the gentle path.
>
> For my heart's desire
> Unto Thine is bent.
> I aspire
> To a full consent.
>
> Not a word or look
> I affect to own,
> But by book,
> And Thy book alone.
>
> Though I fail, I weep.
> Though I halt in pace,
> Yet I creep
> To the throne of grace.

Then let wrath remove.
Love will do the deed:
For with love
Stony hearts will bleed.

Love is swift of foot.
Love's a man of war,
And can shoot,
And can hit from far.

Who can 'scape his bow?
That which wrought on Thee,
Brought Thee low,
Needs must work on me.

Throw away Thy rod,
Though man frailties hath,
Thou art God.
Throw away Thy wrath.

Here there is practically no development of thought; the pathos of the poem is achieved by the very completeness of the mood of trusting humility. Here is a sonnet by Henry Howard, Earl of Surrey, which likewise repeats the idea to strengthen the mood, and works up to an expected climax:

Set me whereas the sun doth parch the green,
Or where his beams do not dissolve the ice;
In temperate heat, where he is felt and seen;
In presence prest of people, mad or wise;
Set me in high, or yet in low degree;
In longest night, or in the shortest day;
In clearest sky, or where clouds thickest be;

In lusty youth, or when my hairs are grey;
Set me in heaven, in earth, or else in hell,
In hill, or dale, or in the foaming flood;
Thrall, or at large, alive whereso I dwell,
Sick, or in health, in evil fame or good,
Hers will I be; and only with this thought
Content myself, although my chance be nought.

On the other hand, a poem may break into two sections with
two ideas antithetical to one another. I do not necessarily mean
a direct contradiction, but a contrast only.

She is not fair to outward view
As many maidens be,
Her loveliness I never knew
Until she smiled on me;
Oh! then I saw her eye was bright,
A well of love, a spring of light.

But now her looks are coy and cold,
To mine they ne'er reply,
And yet I cease not to behold
The love-light in her eye;
Her very frowns are fairer far
Than smiles of other maidens are.

HARTLEY COLERIDGE

Nay but you, who do not love her,
Is she not pure gold, my mistress?
Holds earth aught—speak truth—above her?
Aught like this tress, see, and this tress,
And this last fairest tress of all,
So fair, see, ere I let it fall?

Because you spend your lives in praising;
To praise, you search the wide world over:
Then why not witness, calmly gazing,
If earth holds aught—speak truth—above her?
Above this tress, and this, I touch
But cannot praise, I love so much!

ROBERT BROWNING

Or here is a more direct contradiction from Sir Philip Sidney;
I quote the first and last verses only, as the second and third
verses are allegorical enlargements upon the first:

Ring out you bells, let mourning shows be spread;
For Love is dead:
All Love is dead, infected
With plague of deep disdain:
Worth, as naught worth, rejected,
And Faith fair scorn doth gain.
From so ungrateful fancy,
From such a female frenzy,
From them that use me thus,
Good Lord, deliver us!

.   .   .   .

Alas, I lie: rage hath this error bred;
Love is not dead;
Love is not dead, but sleepeth
In her unmatched mind,
Where she his counsel keepeth,
Till due deserts she find.
Therefore, from so vile fancy,
To call such wit a frenzy,
Who Love can temper thus,
Good Lord, deliver us!

These poems may or may not be more beautiful, but for intellectual experience they are much fuller than the previous pair. Sonnets very often have this kind of contrast in them; the student should examine some of Shakespeare's sonnets; I do not quote any of these, as they ought to be available on everyone's bookshelf. In general, the poem of a single main idea tends rather to make us share the emotion with the writer, the poem of contrast rather to make us join the writer in thinking about the subject; but, like all generalizations, this can be misleading.

The third and most complicated kind of intellectual structure is what might be called dialectical, or a contradiction resolved. Let me illustrate this idea frivolously and crudely, so that I need not pull a beautiful example to pieces:

I am very fond of good food, and am, as might be expected, somewhat fatter than I would wish to be. I sometimes cut down my food in order to lose some of my excess fat. It will be imagined that this sometimes gives rise to mental conflict, and, though the theme is not important enough to give rise to great creative stresses and strains, I can write about it. If I think, now, of food, my first reaction is to contemplate the prospect with delight:

> O how I love to sit and eat
> Hors-d'oeuvres and soup and fish and meat
> With vegetables, then a sweet!
> O what a treat!

Here is a *Rhapsody before Lunch*.[1] I will now add another verse, thus making the poem into the second type, the poem of contrast or contradiction:

[1] Not, I had better add, my usual lunch!

113

> But as I gaze upon my plate
> I know it is my hapless fate,
> Eating, to do the thing I hate,
> To put on weight!

Instead of calling it *Rhapsody before Lunch*, I shall now call it *The Glutton's Dilemma*. The poem still has unity in the contrast, but unity of quite a different kind. Now, if I think the paltry subject of my shape is worth so much attention, I may choose to add a third verse suggesting one of the three possible solutions to the dilemma—to choose grace, to choose grub, or to decide that current ideas of beauty are wrong and to resign myself to my size. Whatever solution I choose, the poem will then be an arrangement of ideas that could be symbolized by the equation $a + b = c$.

> Pass me a second butter-pat!
> I know I never shall be flat!
> I choose to eat although I'm fat,
> And that is that!

This is not a real poem on any usual definition, but I hope it makes clear what I mean by a dialectical arrangement. Such a poem will not, of course, necessarily, be a poem of three verses or even lines in some multiple of three; the same space is not always given to each idea. For further examples the student may like to look at Shakespeare's Sonnets numbers VII, XIX, XXXIII, XLVIII, XCI and CX. Here is a beautiful example from Henry Vaughan:

The Shower

'Twas so; I saw thy birth. That drowsy lake
From her faint bosom breathed thee, the disease
Of her sick waters and infectious ease.

But now at even,
Too gross for Heaven,
Thou fall'st in tears, and weep'st for thy mistake.

Ah! it is so with me. Oft have I pressed
Heaven with a lazy breath, but fruitless this
Pierced not; love only can with quick access
Unlock the way,
When all else stray,
The smoke and exhalations of the breast.

Yet, if as thou dost melt, and with thy train
Of drops make soft the Earth, my eyes could weep
O'er my hard heart, that's bound up and asleep;
Perhaps at last,
Some such showers past,
My God would give a sunshine after rain.

This kind of highly logical structure is most likely to be found
in the 'metaphysical' poets of the seventeenth century, of
whom Henry Vaughan and John Donne are two, and in some
of the best contemporary poets, who have a good deal in
common with the 'metaphysicals', having some of the same
intellectual toughness.

XIII. MENTAL FORM

THE USE OF ASSOCIATIONS

I never see thy face but I think upon hell-fire and Dives that lived in purple; for there he is in his robes, burning, burning.
SHAKESPEARE: *Henry IV*, Pt. 1

EARLY discussion of poetry almost entirely omitted the the study of the effect of associations, and it is only in comparatively recent years that any attempt has been made to study them as systematically as, say, prosody has been studied. Yet they are very important features of poetry.

Much of our learning is done by association of one object or idea with another; all students find that lists of unrelated facts are far harder to learn than groups of related facts. If you wish to remember something, you may tie a knot in your handkerchief, in the hope that every time you take out your handkerchief to blow your nose you will be reminded of your unaccomplished task. If you have to remember some fact such as a date, you will remember it far more easily by making up a jingle about it; and if you cannot think where you put your fountain pen, your best way to find it is probably to think quietly about the events of the day until some train of thought leads you to where you last had the pen.

Associations also have great power to arouse emotions, a fact which makes them, at times, highly dangerous; the cunning use of associations is behind most advertising, much electioneering and a great deal of successful emotional tyranny at home and further afield. Certain words, such as *England*, *family*, *love*, *peace*, *God*, *freedom*, *moral*, may be so heavily loaded with emotion for us that we are unable to consider problems in whose context these words are mentioned without becoming highly unreasonable and intolerant. On the other hand, some words are not easy to pronounce in public because the associations are painful, sordid or embarrassing. If you mention fly-paper to someone whose sole experience of fly-paper is for catching flies, there will be no emotional reaction; but if you mentioned it to someone who a few hours before had publicly been caught by the hair in a fly-paper and made to look foolish, they are likely to blush; if you had the opportunity of mentioning it before someone who had so far successfully concealed a murder committed with arsenic soaked off fly-papers, it would not be surprising if they fainted. The three patterns of association in the individual mind would be quite different.

Association in poetry must obviously depend for its effect on things that are common to many people, not things that are suggested to a very few individuals only. Indeed, a poem is sometimes spoilt by a wrong association due to some change in the meaning of a word. I hope I may be forgiven for admitting that the line:

As if the earth in fast thick pants were breathing

from *Kubla Khan*, used to give me, not the intended picture of a great heaving globe, but a picture of an earth something like the world-on-little-legs of the cartoonists, looking hot and uncomfortable in over-substantial underclothes![1] Fortunately,

---

[1] The reader of poetry should dismiss all such inappropriate associations. The teacher, however, has to watch for them!

a great many associations are to be found in most minds that are sufficiently intelligent and well-furnished to have any associations at all. People of very low intelligence do not enjoy poetry anyway.

A great deal of the effect of poetry depends on these mental connections. If I speak of a *lily*, it suggests purity, but nowadays, thanks to the pictures of the pre-Raphaelites and to Gilbert and Sullivan's *Patience*, it may also suggest a rather sickly, over-refined kind of purity that is more decadent than honest earthiness. 'Cold lilies' would be a safer phrase than 'sweet lilies'. If I speak of a mouse, the atmosphere is one of smallness, friendliness and probably triviality. That is why Falstaff talking to his recruits is so comical when he addresses Feeble, who has said bravely: 'I will do my good will, sir; you can have no more.' 'Well said, good woman's tailor! Well said, courageous Feeble! thou wilt be as valiant as the wrathful dove or the most magnanimous mouse.'—*Henry IV*, part II.

On the other hand, if I mention slimy slugs and writhing worms, the reader is prepared for something revolting.

A woman's hair, if long and healthy, is beautiful, and is fascinating to most men, yet it is not luminous, nor even very bright by reflection; but when Lovelace says:

> Do not then wind up that light
> In ribbands, and o'ercloud in night
> Like the sun in's early ray;
> But shake your head, and scatter day!

we are given, by the associations of brilliant daybreak, a mental picture of a beautiful woman shaking out a mass of golden locks so radiantly bright that they seem to be dripping with golden light. It is a lovely image, though true only for a lover.

The same word does not always carry the same associations, and may carry two or more associations at once; the latter is often very important in some of the most exciting poetry. *Blood* can mean 'rank', 'aristocracy':

> The glories of our blood and state
> Are shadows, not substantial things. . . .
>
> > SHIRLEY

> A shielded scutcheon blush'd with blood of queens and
>   kings.
>
> > KEATS

It can instead mean 'murder', 'War', 'atrocity':

> It will have blood, they say; blood will have blood;
> Stones have been known to move and trees to speak;
> Augurs and understood relations have
> By maggot-pies and choughs and rooks brought forth
> The secret'st man of blood.
>
> > SHAKESPEARE: *Macbeth*

It can suggest human lust and the instinctive life—we know the phrase 'hot blood' for the part of our lives during which, if healthy, we are liable to fall in love:

> I do know
> When the blood burns, how prodigal the soul
> Lends the tongue vows. . . .
>
> > SHAKESPEARE: *Hamlet*

and it can, in two lines only, horribly suggest both at once:

> Oh, my greatest sin lay in my blood!
> Now my blood pays for't.
>
> > WEBSTER: *The White Devil*

The word can also be divorced from its associations of death and evil to suggest the flush on the face of a young girl:

> Hood my unmanned blood, bating in my cheeks. . . .
> SHAKESPEARE: *Romeo and Juliet*

Roses suggest love and a certain softness or luxuriance; gold suggests riches, hardness or prestige; purple may suggest rank, or sacrifice, authority or blood or mourning; green is the colour of Spring and hope or in some contexts may remind us instead of the ugly colours of putrefaction; the sun is generally beneficent:

> The sun, whose beams most glorious are
> Rejecteth no beholder. . . .

> Sun of my soul, thou Saviour dear. . . .

but can also be sinister when associated with the deadly sun of the desert:

> The sun says, 'I will suck your bones
> And afterwards bury you.'
> SIDNEY KEYES: *The Wilderness*

The associations of a word thus depend very largely on the context. Words like *roses, blood, wine, bread, hair, hands, stars, bells, worms, home, mother*, that are in everyday use and heavily charged with associations are more likely to be effective in poetry than such words as *iambic, pethidine, mollusc, rotation, detergent, hydrogen, matriculation*, whose meaning is so sharply defined that there is little room for a haze of associations around them. On the other hand, every now and then the poetic language becomes tedious from overmuch use of stock words, and a reaction takes place; some words become un-fashionable and new words are brought in to refresh the lan-guage. This is entirely as it should be; the contemporary poets of the more intellectual type, such as Auden, Kathleen Raine, Day Lewis, William Empson, and T. S. Eliot himself, have done a tremendous service to English poetry by widening its vocabulary.

French, and to a lesser extent English, classicist critics such as Samuel Johnson tried to teach writers that there were limitations on the vocabulary proper to poetry, imposed by considerations of dignity. When a translation of *Othello* was first performed in France, the word *mouchoir* (handkerchief) nearly provoked a riot; so common an object was quite be-neath the dignity of poetry and should have been mentioned in a long-winded circumlocution. Shakespeare has been blamed for making Heaven, in *Macbeth*, *peep* through the *blanket* of the dark, on the grounds that this was undignified. The idea that some words were more suited to poetry than others was probably an early consciousness of the power of a word's associations, and there is enough truth in it to make its acceptance understandable. The handkerchief of Desdemona and the 'blanket of the dark' are acceptable enough to us, but the best of poets would still have some difficulty in introducing such a word as *kippers* or *peanuts* into a poem that was lyrical without humour or irony.[1] Nowadays it is safer to say that all words are suitable for use in poetry, however crude and common, rare, or technical, provided that their associations are appropriate to the context or, if they have a number of different associations, that the force of the context is sufficient to keep the unwanted ones out of our minds. On the whole—

[1] Louis MacNeice has successfully used many words such as *peanuts, pretzels, beer, clams, queues,* in his fine ironical poem *Bar-Room Matins.*

if we are to judge from literary history—anything that narrows the scope of poetry is likely to be a mistake.

This importance of associations is one of the principal differences between prose and poetry; I am not sure that it is not more important even than the use of metrical pattern. All metaphor depends on associations, and metaphor is the very life of poetry; metaphor (and kindred modes of speech such as simile and personification) is imagery. We do reason in prose by analogy, which is a kind of simile:

'If you exercise your mind with literature, philosophy and science, it will grow broader and more able, just as if you exercise your body muscles will develop and you will be stronger.'

'A spiral staircase is one that goes round and round like a corkscrew, instead of up at an angle.'

But such explanations are useful only to help us to understand the fact; they are not emotionally exciting. Analogy in reasoning elucidates; metaphor in poetry enriches. We may already know the fact; indeed, if we do not we shall probably not gain the maximum excitement from the poem; but something is added to our experience by seeing it expressed in an image. No one needs to be told that time flies fast and that we never have time enough to do all we wish; but when we read Marvell's great lines:

> But at my back I always hear
> Time's winged chariot hurrying near;
> And yonder all before us lie
> Desarts of vast eternity.

it does add something to our sense of urgency. Here is a simile —the simplest form of image—used by Landor to elucidate, actually to make us see something in a new light.

On Catullus
Tell me not what too well I know
About the bard of Sirmio. . . .
Yes, in Thalia's son
Such stains there are . . . as when a Grace
Sprinkles another's laughing face
With nectar, and runs on.

This is very like the use of analogy in prose; yet the choice of words, making a picture, enriches the idea. The vices of Catullus, which were sensual, are attributed by association to pagan vitality and placed in a setting of fresh youth and beauty. The sensual vices (so-called) are not repulsive in the young and beautiful, so we feel we can accept this explanation, though in cold fact it is no explanation at all.

Let us take a short and fairly simple lyric and study the use of associations in it:

Music, when soft voices die,
Vibrates in the memory—
Odours, when sweet violets sicken,
Live within the sense they quicken.

Rose leaves, when the rose is dead,
Are heaped for the beloved's bed;
And so thy thoughts when thou art gone,
Love itself shall slumber on.

SHELLEY

Now, if we are to consider merely the rational meaning of this, it is platitudinous: 'We are able to recollect the experiences of listening to music and smelling violets; dead roses can be used in the house; in some such way, when you are gone, your thoughts will be something on which Love can rest.'

This is sorry stuff and has lost all the wistfulness and grace of the poem.

The poem suggests far more than it says, Its title is *To* ——, evidently one of the women idealistically loved by Shelley. The music is vocal music, which is more intimately personal than instrumental music; the 'soft voice' is part of a woman's physical attraction, especially for a refined and spiritual man such as Shelley; indeed, the use of the word 'soft' suggests that the poet is thinking of speech as much as music, for too soft a voice is useless for singing. Violets are associated with modesty and fragrance and are a flower made more precious by needing to be sought. (We can also think of the violets in Donne's *The Exstasie* and the 'beds of violets blue and fresh-blown roses washed in dew' of Milton; the violet had earlier literary associations of love and happiness.) 'Sicken' is a more human word than 'wither'; it suggests almost that the withering of violets is not necessary, that it is an illness rather than the normal state of things, or else, conversely, we may take it to mean that our illnesses and death and the disillusionments of love are like the fading of flowers, natural and easy. The rose is very rich with associations of love, happiness and festivity:

> For nothing this wide universe I call
> Save thee, my rose; in it thou art my all.
>
> SHAKESPEARE

> It was roses, roses, all the way.
>
> BROWNING

The rose leaves could just as well, factually, have gone into a jar to make fragrant pot-pourri, and indeed the cynic might argue that rose leaves would not be comfortable in bed; but the 'bed' is used to suggest some kind of loving ritual (as with altar flowers, perhaps?) and to take up the picture of Love slumbering. The suggestion of Love slumbering is also that Love may again be awakened. If we take into account all these associations and implications the poem becomes much more subtle and beautiful.

In order to be effective, associations must be generally comprehensible. Everyone agrees that roses, violets and music are agreeable things. Sometimes when a reader does not appreciate a poem fully it is because some of the associations are not affecting him. This may be the poet's fault for using associations that even an educated and sensitive person cannot be expected to grasp. More often it is the fault of circumstance because the association has become unfamiliar with the passage of time, or is not now emotionally charged. More often still it is the reader's fault for having inadequate general knowledge, experience, or imagination. It is, I think, the business of a poet to choose images that are comprehensible to his audience[1] if he wants an audience. But it should be added that the poet has a perfect right to choose his audience. T. S. Eliot and Robert Burns are both very fine poets; Eliot demands a much higher standard of culture from his readers; but he is entirely justified in writing for a smaller audience. There will always be some people too stupid, lazy or ignorant to enjoy any poem, even a simple one; the poet is expected merely to avoid making impossible demands on the kind of audience for which he is writing. (In a sense the poet is always writing mostly to himself; but if we are studying his work it must have been published, which implies that he wishes for some audience.)

Let me again take a flippant example. I am very short-

[1] Not always intellectually, in the sense that the poem can be paraphrased word-for-word; the morning-bright Apollo forbid so narrow an idea of 'understanding'!

sighted, and am helpless without the glasses I wear all day. Suppose I wished to write a poem of dignity and pathos about some terrible political problem with which my country was faced, and how difficult it was to see what to do; I might, drawing a vital image from my own daily experience, say something like this:

> Confused as is the room to waking eyes,
> Early, before the spectacles are on,
> The borders blurred, the detail indistinct,
> All dangers seeming larger than they are. . . .

This is an excellent image for *me*; but for someone who has faultless eyesight and has never experienced a blurring of vision it is nearly meaningless. Actually ordinary human sympathy probably extends so far; most people are aware of the predicaments of spectacle-wearers; but the image would lack all the vividness and realism it has for me. Everybody has at some time looked out through a rain-smeared window on to a dark night, and it would be much better to say, using an image that is intelligible both to the normally sighted and to me, that is therefore successful as *communication*:

> Confused as darkening gardens are outside,
> When heavy rain channels the window pane,
> And all the trees take on a sinister size
> In blurs and gathering opacity.

I have said that we must be careful not to put a word in a context where it carries the inappropriate associations, but some of the most exciting associations may very well be ambiguous. One of the continually exciting things about life is that everything is a part of everything else, and associations in poetry often heighten this awareness. For example, in Andrew Marvell's *The Garden* we find these two lines:

> When we have run our passion's heat,
> Love hither makes his best retreat.

There is a surprising amount of implication packed into these two lines. 'Heat' is here obviously a heat in a race, since we 'run' it; we have finished that part of our life in which passion is important. But passion is itself, in literary parlance, 'heat', both in a refined metaphorical sense and as when we speak of an animal being 'in heat'. 'Retreat' suggests defeat in battle— Love surrenders, gives in, to the inevitable; but it also suggests, and would probably do so much more strongly to the very religion-conscious seventeenth century, a religious 're- treat'—a retirement from the world to monastery or convent in order to contemplate. Thus the couplet has four possible meanings and all of them are really to be felt together. To pursue such ambiguous associations is a very exciting part of criticism.

Association can also be used ironically. Wilfred Owen, in his poems of protest at the horror and cruelty of war, fre- quently does this, as here, describing a young boy with a gun:

> Lend him to stroke those blind, blunt bullet-heads
> Which long to nuzzle in the hearts of lads.

'Stroke' and 'nuzzle' suggest an affectionate relationship with a pet, and the implications are that the boy ought to be playing with harmless pets rather than familiarizing himself with lethal weapons, also that he is making a pet of his gun, treating it as a toy because he is too young to understand his situation.

The sting of satire is often sharpened by the use of association, even though completely unfair. Byron in *English Bards and Scotch Reviewers* writes of Wordsworth:

> Thus, when he tells the tale of Betty Foy,
> The idiot mother of 'an idiot boy';
> A moon-struck, silly lad, who lost his way,
> And like his bard confounded night with day;
> So close on each pathetic part he dwells,
> And each adventure so sublimely tells,
> That all who view 'the idiot in his glory'
> Conceive the bard the hero of the story.

Now, this is undoubtedly funny and clever, but it is most unfair, for it manages to imply that Wordsworth is himself an idiot, with no more evidence given than that the poet once wrote a poem about an idiot boy. (It is not even accurate, for the boy's mother was not an idiot.) All the epithets applied to the idiot and his mother are obliquely being flung at Wordsworth himself. Satire is meant to be aggressive and must be allowed to make some rash assumptions and exaggerations; often the less fair satire is the funnier it is; but we must distinguish the real criticism in satire from the clever use of associations and implications.

XIV. MENTAL FORM

THE TWO MAIN PATTERNS OF IMAGERY

> All garlanded with carven imag'ries
> KEATS: *Eve of St. Agnes*

IN general a poem may have a series of images that support or contradict one another, or a single dominant image on which the sequence and structure of the poem depend. Burns's *A Red, Red Rose* expresses passionate love by a series of simple and beautiful hyperboles; his effect is achieved by an accumulation of images that are not closely related to one another.[1]

> O my luve is like a red, red rose,
> That's newly sprung in June;
> O my luve is like the melodie,
> That's sweetly play'd in tune.
>
> As fair art thou, my bonnie lass,
> So deep in luve am I;
> And I will luve thee still, my dear,
> Till a' the seas gang dry.
>
> Till a' the seas gang dry, my dear,
> And the rocks melt wi' the sun;

[1] The student who has read the previous chapter attentively will find much food for thought in the associations.

And I will love thee still, my dear,
While the sand o' life shall run.

And fare-thee-weel, my only luve!
And fare-thee-weel awhile!
And I will come again, my luve,
Though it were ten thousand mile.

Collections of unrelated images may also be found in Nashe's *Adieu; farewell Earth's bliss*, Crashaw's *Wishes for the Supposed Mistress*, and Shelley's *When the Lamp is Shattered*.

Another type of poem, which makes a very different impression on the mind, uses a single central, dominant image and builds the whole structure of the poem around it. In George Herbert's *Love* the experience of divine love is shown as the shy attendance of a consciously unworthy guest at a feast:

Love bade me welcome; yet my soul drew back,
Guilty of dust and sin.
But quick-eyed Love, observing me grow slack
From my first entrance in,
Drew nearer to me, sweetly questioning
If I lacked anything.

A guest, I answered, worthy to be here.
Love said, You shall be he.
I, the unkind, ungrateful? Ah, my dear,
I cannot look on thee.
Love took my hand and smiling made reply,
Who made the eyes but I?

Truth, Lord, but I have marred them; let my shame
Go where it doth deserve.

And know you not, says Love, who bore the blame?
My dear, then I will serve.
You must sit down, said Love, and taste my meat.
So I did sit and eat.

This is, in a sense, a small allegory, though the term is more often given to a larger piece of work. Clearly, here, Love is Divine Love, probably Christ as Redeemer, and the unworthy guest is George Herbert, aware of his sins; but we need not try to find allegorical meanings for the taking of the hand or the making of the eyes; ''twere to consider too curiously, to consider so.' It is possible that the poem refers to the actual partaking of the Holy Communion, but it might equally well be a poem about some other mystical experience of God outside orthodox ritual. I, who am not a Christian, can still be moved by its beauty, because I know that even human love, at its best, is like this, this unconditional generosity of spirit that takes no notice of our deserving. The refusal to produce images which are very limited in their application has probably widened the audience that can appreciate the poem.

An image may also recur in a long poem or a dramatic poem so often as to be its dominant image; its choice is very significant. It has been pointed out that this is often true of the plays of Shakespeare: the image of torture and physical cruelty recurs in *King Lear*; darkness and blood in *Macbeth*; disease in *Hamlet*; animals and the sea in *Othello*. The relationship of these dominant images to the plot is obvious.

Many poets have favourite images that recur in their poems. Shelley's works are full of friendly snakes, the sea and the sky; the poems of Donne, more earthy and more rational, are full of images drawn from science and theology. Wordsworth has a powerful favourite symbol of some solitary figure in impressive natural surroundings—the Leech Gatherer, Lucy Gray, the soldier in *The Prelude*; Keats is full of images of texture, colour and sensation. In the poems of A. E. Housman a hanging frequently plays a part, though we know of no biographical reason. W. H. Auden has images of children, Roy Campbell of red, violence, and the beasts and birds of South Africa; James Kirkup favours the sea and mirrors; spindles and gyres turn among the gold and blood of W. B. Yeats and at one time C. Day Lewis was using much imagery drawn from railways. The student should look out for other examples. This is usually because poets create their own personal mythology. Similarly many poets have favourite words that recur with sometimes embarrassing frequency: Shelley's *skiey* and *crystal*, Swinburne's *roses* and *tears* and *sin*, Pope's *wit*, Blake's *howling*, Wordsworth's *solitary*, give a clue to their interests.

This is not merely, however, evidence of the general capacity of human beings for repeating themselves. The poet chooses an image to illustrate his own experience for himself, as well as to pass it on to others. The imagery of a poem is often not so much like a pattern chosen for embroidery or the few well-chosen words arranged for a public speech, as like a myth or the illogical but curiously exciting pictures seen in dreams. I once heard a distinguished young woman biologist read some poetry that she had written; it was quite good poetry, though she refused to publish it; she read it with sincerity and then rejected it with scorn, saying that the images were all the usual dream-symbols mentioned by Freud. This was true, but did not seem to me to spoil her poems. Various students of literature who are also psychologists have pointed out the resemblance of much poetic language to dreams, myths and the visionary experiences of primitive men.[1] The poet does not always consciously choose his image; the image may choose him. The psychologist will say that an image that insists on being used has sprung from the unconscious mind; the romantic idealist will say that the poet is divinely inspired. On this difference of opinion I can do no better than quote the great wisdom of George Bernard Shaw, who, when the Inquisitors tell Saint Joan that the 'voices' she hears come from her imagination, makes her say: 'Of course; that is how the messages of God come to us.' When a poet has an obvious dominant personal image, the psychologist can usually suggest a reason, but this does not make the poem any less good. In general, it seems that the poems that are most widely appreciated are those whose images are present in the minds of most people. A poem depicting the forces of evil as a great snake would be accepted by most Westerners; a poem of equal artistic merit depicting them as an enormous frog might not be accepted so readily.

Sometimes we feel the effect of a poem more by relaxing and letting it sink in than by studying it intellectually. This is true of much of Swinburne, Shelley, Blake, Poe, Whitman and Spenser. The images affect us long before we have grasped the intellectual meaning. I have a curious little memory of this. As a quite small child, I think of about eight, I read *A Midsummer Night's Dream* and was so terrified by the lines:

> I'll believe as soon
> The whole earth may be bor'd, and that the moon
> May through the centre creep, and so displease
> Her brother's noontide with the Antipodes.

[1] See Herbert Read: 'Myth, Dream and Poem' in his *Collected Literary Criticism.*

that I lay awake at night with obscure pictures of darkness and horror multiplying in my head. *A Midsummer Night's Dream* is not the play one would hesitate to give to little girls! But, with no understanding of 'antipodes' and not much understanding of the words at all, I did receive some disturbingly strong impression of the whole order of Nature being upset. I still find the idea terrifying now that I know what it means, and occasionally have dreams of double suns, distorted moons and strange new features in the sky. However, probably a really great poem is one in which the image, while it has an immediate and powerful emotional effect, will also bear intellectual analysis. In Otway's *Venice Preserved* the heroine goes mad and makes an exit speaking incoherently of

> Lutes, laurels, seas of milk and ships of amber.

This is reasonable enough to suggest the ravings of a stage madwoman; it makes no sense, it sounds pleasant and the vague suggestion of glory, music and plenty is suitable to the high rank of the personages. Yet, compared with the ravings of Lear, this seems poor, synthetic stuff. The student should turn to *King Lear*, Act IV, scene vi, and examine Lear's mad speeches in detail. Every image, pretty, grandiose or repulsive, has significance; minute intellectual analysis of its implications (including the stage business implied) is possible. For the greatest poetic excitement, we need imagery that shall strike directly at the unconscious mind and also be worth analysis by the conscious reasoning mind.

At one time it seems likely that poets gave very much less conscious thought to their images than they do to-day. Allegory was, of course, worked out in minute detail and with great care; massive epic similes provided 'purple patches'; but some of the most exciting images of early poetry give the

impression of having been discovered almost by accident; they
have the dew upon them:

> He cam all so stille
> As his mother lay
> As dew in Aprille
> That falles on the spray.
>
> Old Carol

> Brightness falls from the air.
>
> NASHE

> The maid she went to the well to washe,
> Dew fell off her lily-white flesh.
>
> Ballad

> Then Mary plucked a cherry
> As red as the blood;
> Then Mary went home
> With her heavy load.
>
> Old Carol

> More pale she was, when she sought my grace,
> Than primrose pale and wan;
> And redder than rose her ruddy heart's blood
> That down my broadsword ran.
>
> *Jellon Graeme*

> O the wind is longer nor the way
> And love is deeper nor the sea.
>
> *The Riddling Knight*

> Sing levy dew, sing levy dew,
> The water and the wine;
> The seven bright gold wires
> And the bugles they do shine.
>
> A New Year Carol

The student might also think of the queer excitement of the full version of *Green Grow the Rushes-O* with its half-understood primitive symbols, *Maiden in the Moor Lay*, and this nursery rhyme, not now much used among children:

> This is the Key of the Kingdom:
> In that Kingdom is a city;
> In that city is a town;
> In that town there is a street;
> In that street there winds a lane;
> In that lane there is a yard;
> In that yard there is a house;
> In that house there waits a room;
> In that room an empty bed;
> And on that Bed a basket—
> A Basket of Sweet Flowers,
> Of Flowers, of Flowers,
> A Basket of Sweet Flowers.
>
> Flowers in a Basket;
> Basket on the bed;
> Bed in the chamber;
> Chamber in the house;
> House in the weedy yard;
> Yard in the winding lane;
> Lane in the broad street;
> Street in the high town;
> Town in the city;
> City in the Kingdom;
> This is the Key of the Kingdom,
> Of the Kingdom this is the Key.

A whole chapter could be given to commenting upon this amazing poem; completely unsophisticated and having very possibly happened by 'accident', it has some symbols of great richness.

Nowadays all poets must surely give some conscious thought to their images. It could be argued that after the intellectual power of Milton, Donne and Dryden, and the even more conscious intellectuality but lesser depth of Pope and his disciples, the Romantic Revival was an attempt to return to spontaneity in image-finding; it is noticeable that many poetic revolutions appeal to the idea of 'Back to Nature'. Civilized modern man has a sense of having lost something. People who criticize late twentieth-century poets for being over-intellectual, over-self-conscious, may be explaining successfully why this poetry does not appeal to them, but offer no solution to the problem of how to write with spontaneity when we know a good deal about all the various forces—chemical, physical, psychological, economic, social—that govern our lives, shape our destinies and help to create our personalities. I myself imagine that the eventual development of English poetry will be, like the third kind of poem described by me in Chapter XII, dialectical: the poet will be born, or is now perhaps a schoolboy or schoolgirl, for whom our contemporary knowledge that makes for self-consciousness will be taken so much for granted as to be like the seasons and the ages of man to more primitive poets.[1] We have certainly not nearly exhausted the mystery, interestingness and the endless wonder of life upon earth; those who hate science as taking away the beauty and mystery of life have either never looked

[1] Hugh Macdiarmid in Scotland has probably come as near as anyone to attempting such a synthesis, not without some measure of success.

down a microscope, up a telescope or into a work of modern psychology, or are incapable of feeling awe anyway and are merely sentimental over the sweet mysteries of life.

XV. SOME TRADITIONAL VERSE FORMS

Set in a notebook, learned and conn'd by rote . .
SHAKESPEARE: *Julius Caesar*

THERE is no great merit in learning all the traditional forms of verse; this is the kind of knowledge that resembles philately rather than philosophy; but a list may be useful for reference by examination candidates, and this seems to be a suitable place to put it.

1. *Blank Verse*

Definition: A sequence of unrhymed iambic pentameters.[1] There is no need to give an example, as I assume that anyone reading this book has access to the plays of Shakespeare and to Milton's *Paradise Lost*. This is the principal verse form for dramatic poetry in English and is also a favourite form for the long poem. It is very flexible and can be very dignified. It is also the nearest traditional verse form to normal human speech.

2. *Heroic Couplet*

Definition: Iambic pentameter lines rhyming in pairs. Although termed 'heroic' the form is most commonly used in English for satirical or didactic poetry. It was a favoured

[1] IMPORTANT: These examination definitions give only the *basic* metre.

form in the eighteenth century, but has never gone entirely out of fashion.

Examples: Pope, *Essay on Criticism*; Byron, *Hints from Horace*; Johnson, *The Vanity of Human Wishes*; Skinner, *Letters to Malaya*.

3. Sonnet

Definition: A poem of fourteen iambic pentameter lines, with one of the following rhyme-schemes:
Shakespearian: abab cdcd efef gg.
Petrarchan or Italian: abba abba cde cde *or* abba abba ccd eed. There is usually a break in the sense between the octave (first eight lines) and sestet (last six lines) or, in the Shakespearian sonnet, the only break is sometimes before the final couplet. There are several other variations of the rhyme scheme.

4. Tailed Sonnet

Definition: A normal sonnet to which some extra lines have been added, giving the reader a surprise. This is not common in English; the best known is Milton's *On the New Forces of Conscience under the Long Parliament*. This is a Petrarchan sonnet followed by a trimeter, two pentameters, a trimeter and two pentameters, rhyming cfffgg. It is more common in Italian poetry. G. M. Hopkins also uses this form.

5. Terza Rima

Definition: Iambic pentameters rhyming aba bcb cdc ded efe and so on, ending with a quatrain or couplet to avoid leaving one word unrhymed. The form is taken from Dante's *Divina Commedia*. It is not very common in English poetry.

Examples: Byron, *The Prophecy of Dante* (appropriately!); Shelley, *The Triumph of Life*, *Ode to the West Wind*, *Prince Athanase*.

6. Ottava Rima

Definition: Eight (*ottava*) iambic pentameters rhyming ababbcc. This attractive narrative form is found in several well-known English poems.

Examples: Byron, *Don Juan*, *Beppo*; Keats, *Isabella*.

7. Spenserian Stanza

Definition: Eight iambic pentameters followed by one iambic hexameter (Alexandrine) and rhyming ababbcbcc. Probably the most ornate and splendid English verse-form to be found in narrative poems.

Examples: Spenser, *The Faerie Queene*; Byron, *Childe Harold's Pilgrimage*; Shelley, *The Revolt of Islam*; Keats, *The Eve of St. Agnes*.

8. The 'Troilus' Stanza or Rhyme Royal

Definition: Seven iambic pentameters rhyming ababbcc. This stanza is used by Chaucer in his magnificent narrative poem *Troilus and Criseyde*, a great novel in verse that, having been eclipsed by the *Canterbury Tales*, is less well known than it deserves to be.

Examples: Chaucer, *The Clerk's Tale*; Auden, *Letter to Lord Byron*.

9. Ballade (not to be confused with *ballad*)

Definition: Three stanzas of eight or ten lines each, with four or five lines at the end, known as the *envoy*, using three or four rhymes only in the same order in each stanza and with exactly the same line concluding each stanza and the envoy. Several basic metres have been used.

Examples: Chaucer, *Lak of Stedfastnesse*, *Balade de bon conseyl* (or *Truth*); Chesterton, *A Ballade of Suicide*, *A Ballade of the First Rain*; Austin Dobson, *The Pompadour's Fan*; Michael Scot, *Ballade of the Cats of Bygone Time*.

In England this very difficult verse form has never been much more than a technical exercise, what might be called 'drawing-room poetry'; but just across the Channel François Villon wrote several Ballades which are among the world's greatest poems.

10. *Rondeau, and its variants*

Definition: A short poem in which the opening words recur at stated places and only two rhymes are used. A strict *rondeau* has thirteen lines; a *Rondeau of Villon* has ten; a *Rondel* has fourteen or thirteen lines; the term *Roundel* may be applied to either a rondeau or a rondel, but it is also used by Swinburne for a poem of nine lines and two refrains.[1] Like the Ballade, this is a highly artificial form generally used for trivial 'drawing-room' verse.

Examples: Swinburne, '*A roundel is wrought . . .*'; Villon, *Jenin l'Avenu, Repos eternel donne à cil, Au retour de dure prison, Mort, j'appelle de ta rigueur*. (Translations of these will be found in a book of Villon's Ballades, selected by Andre Deutsch and Mervyn Savill and published by Allan Wingate.) The best English rondeaux are the more serious ones by Sir Thomas Wyatt, and the three by Chaucer in the set called *Merciles Beaute*.

11. *Triolet*

Definition: An eight-line poem in which the second line is used twice and the first three times and only two rhymes are used.

Example: Bridges, *All women born are so perverse. . . .* Another very artificial form, used chiefly for light playful poems.

[1] For the details of this definition I am indebted to Fowler's *Modern English Usage*.

12. *Villanelle*

Definition: Five (sometimes more) sets of three lines (tercets) ending with a quatrain, using two rhymes only and repeating the first line at the end of the second and fourth tercet, the third line at the end of the first, third and fifth tercets; the final quatrain ends with the first and third lines.

Example: Austin Dobson, *When I saw you last, Rose*. . . . A highly artificial form, so repetitive that it generally says very little.

In English the last four forms are seldom serious and are often irritating; because of their technical complexity they take up an amount of space in a reference book quite out of all proportion to their importance. They are, however, to be recommended as exercises to any young poet who wants to master the technicalities of versification. There has been a recent revival of this form for serious purposes, as in William Empson's *Missing Dates* and poems by Auden, G. S. Fraser and John Wain.

13. *English Hexameters*

Are to be divided into two quite different forms:

(1) Definition: Iambic hexameters, rhymed or unrhymed.
Examples: Michael Drayton, *Poly-Olbion*; Browning, *Fifine at the Fair*; Bridges, *Testament of Beauty* (loose). This is not a common English form but is a perfectly possible one.

(2) An attempt at imitating in English the effect of Greek and Latin hexameters, the general effect of which is something like English dactyls. As it is difficult to write a poem of any length in English dactyls, and there are no quantities in English, the experiment is generally unsuccessful.

Examples: Longfellow, *Evangeline*; A. H. Clough, *The*

Bothie of Tober-na-Vuolich (one of the best English poems in this form, still worth reading).

During the sixteenth century the distrust of the vernacular as less dignified and durable than the classical languages led to a strong movement for the use of classical metres in English led by such people, more scholars than artists, as Gabriel Harvey. Sidney and other poets made attempts at writing English quantitative verse.

14. Octosyllabics

Definition: Though this logically could mean any kind of eight-syllable line, it is generally applied to iambic tetrameters that rhyme in couplets, which is a useful narrative form in English.

Examples: Butler, *Hudibras*; Scott, *The Lady of the Lake, Marmion*; Marvell, *The Garden* (not narrative); Byron, *The Prisoner of Chillon*; Keats, *The Eve of St. Mark*; Auden, *New Year Letter* (not narrative).

15. Couplets

Definition: Any metre with lines rhyming in pairs.

16. Triplets

Definition: Any metre with lines rhyming in sets of three.
Examples: Tennyson, *The Two Voices*; Kathleen Raine, *Passion*.

17. Quatrains

Definition: Any metre with lines rhyming in sets of four. The possible rhyme schemes are obviously: abab, abcb, aaaa, abba, aaab, aaba.

Some common forms of quatrain are:

(a) 'Common Measure'—the C.M. of the hymn books. Lines alternating eight and six syllables, rhyming abab or abcb. *Examples*: Coleridge, *The Ancient Mariner* (with variations), and many of the old ballads.

(b) 'Long Measure'—the L.M. of the hymn books. Quatrains with eight syllables in every line, rhyming abab or abcb. *Examples*: A number of the ballads; Tennyson, *In Memoriam* (but rhyming abba).

(c) 'Short Measure'—the S.M. of the hymn books. Quatrains of 6.6.8 and 6 syllables, rhyming abab or abcb.

(d) The 'Omar Khayyam' quatrain—iambic pentameter rhyming aaba.

(e) The 'Gondibert' or 'Elegiac' stanza of Gray's *Elegy*.

18. *The Burns Metre*

Definition: A form used by Robert Burns with great success, and not otherwise very common in English, consisting of stanzas of three iambic tetrameters, one dimeter, one tetrameter and one dimeter, rhyming aaabab. Burns was not, however, the originator of the form.

Examples: Burns, *Holy Willie's Prayer*, *To a Mouse*, *Address to a Haggis*.

19. *Chant Royal*

Definition: An extremely elaborate verse-form resembling a ballade but having five stanzas of eleven lines each and an envoy of five or eight lines. Not important in English.

20. *Poulter's Measure*

Definition: Alternating iambic hexameters and seven-foot lines, used a good deal by minor poets of the sixteenth century. This form, which is inclined to drag, can be broken up into Short Measure.

Examples: Nicholas Grimald, *A Truelove*; Queen Elizabeth, *That Daughter of Debate*; Fulke Greville, Lord Brooke, *Epitaph on Sir Philip Sidney*; Nicholas Breton, *Phyllis*. (All these will be found in the *Oxford Book of Sixteenth Century Verse*.)

21. *Rime Couée or Tailed Rhyme*

Definition: Six-line stanzas of two iambic tetrameters and one trimeter, twice, rhyming aabaab. Much used in the early Romances and not much used afterwards.

Example: Chaucer, *Sir Thopas* (an amusing parody).

22. *Sestina*

Definition: An elaborate poem-form borrowed from the Italian, which borrowed it from the invention of the Proven-çal poet Arnaut Daniel. Instead of using rhyme, it uses a repetition of the final words of a line, but altering the order; it consists of six verses with a final triplet. It is not common in English. It has however been used by Drummond, Spenser, Sidney, Swinburne, Kipling, Auden.

Example: Ezra Pound, *Altaforte*.

23. *Skeltonics*

Definition: Short lines with an irregular pattern, but rhyming, as used by John Skelton.

Examples: *Lament for Philip Sparrow*, *The Tunning of Elinor Rumming*.

The intelligent reader will notice that there are hundreds of forms, especially of lyrics, that have no 'official' name. Some of them are far more beautiful than some of the highly artificial forms that have 'official' names.

Modern free verse requires a short chapter to itself, if only as a counterblast to all the conventional syllable-counters who have tried to discredit it.

XVI. FREE VERSE

Bear witness for me, whereso'er ye be,
With what deep worship I have still adored
The spirit of divinest Liberty.
COLERIDGE: *France: An Ode*

THERE has been a great deal of controversy about free verse, and some of the things said on both sides have been exaggerated and ridiculous. Some people think that free verse is a final insult to poetry and call it 'chopped prose'; others think that it is the final liberation of poetry; some suspect that the writers of free verse use it because of inability to use the conventional forms, just as some people who had never seen the early drawings of Picasso said that he used startling experimental techniques because he could not draw. Some young poets no doubt have tried to write free verse out of laziness and a misconception of its nature; but the best writers of free verse, such as Richard Aldington, Herbert Read, Ezra Pound and D. H. Lawrence, have used more traditional forms with dexterity and success. Accusations of lazy writing, sometimes true, are more often admissions of lazy reading that, in looking for one pattern, fails to see another.

Let us consider what free verse is. It is unrhymed verse without a traditional metrical form. The twentieth century has been a period of much innovation in English verse forms, and some of the innovations have been various methods of free verse.[1] There have also been many modifications of the traditional forms, as in the brilliant dramatic verse of T. S. Eliot and Christopher Fry, both of which can be explained by referring to traditional prosody, but do not resemble the rhythms of Marlowe or Shakespeare. Some of the new methods have included: reproduction of normal speech rhythms more exact than is possible within the conventional verse forms (T. S. Eliot, Herbert Read, Ezra Pound, Richard Aldington); an unrhymed verse that nevertheless gives the impression of a highly stylized artificiality, in imitation of Japanese or Chinese poetry (Amy Lowell, Ezra Pound); presenting a single image that is striking in a few unrhymed lines (Herbert Read, T. E. Hulme, Amy Lowell); to use typographical devices as an integral part of the form (E. E. Cummings, José Garcia Villa); and to use unrhymed lines in a strictly symmetrical arrangement with equality of syllables though not of metre (Herbert Read, Marianne Moore). It will be noticed that some of the poets mentioned here are Americans; nowadays movements in poetry generally cover both America and Britain.

Good free verse is not at all easy to write, for there is no repetitive beat to lull the reader's critical faculty. I have always found that the easiest form of which to write a presentable specimen is one of the 'drawing-room' forms—at one time I wrote many ballades to amuse friends. The reader is so much impressed by the 'difficulty' of the form that a few other weaknesses, such as stiff inversions or insincerities, are excused. Next come the usual forms such as sonnet, quatrain and couplet, which flow smoothly. I have never written blank verse with which I have been satisfied, because it is difficult to write it without setting oneself in presumptuous competition with

[1] See Livingstone Lowes: *Convention and Revolt in Poetry*.

Shakespeare and Milton by imitating their habits. Last and hardest of all is free verse, in which the slightest intellectual, psychological or aesthetic failure stands mercilessly exposed.

It would be possible to apply the term 'free verse' to any poem which had no rhyme, other than blank verse which has its individual title; there are the poems written in imitation of classical metres, such as Campion's:

> Rose-cheeked Laura, come;
> Sing thou smoothly with thy beauty's
> Silent music, either other
> Sweetly gracing.
>
> Lovely forms do flow
> From concent divinely framed;
> Heaven is music, and thy beauty's
> Birth is heavenly.
>
> These dull notes we sing
> Discords need for helps to grace them;
> Only beauty purely loving
> Knows no discord;
>
> But still moves delight,
> Like clear springs renewed by flowing,
> Ever perfect, ever in them-
> selves eternal.

or Longfellow's *Hiawatha* in its unrhymed trochaic tetra-meters. Blank verse itself would not have acquired a special title had it not been used by a large number of English poets. It would be equally possible to call any poem which has rhymes but no regular rhythm 'free verse'; examples are the poems of John Skelton, the irregular odes of Cowley and his imitators, once known as 'Pindarics', and the humorous verses of Ogden Nash. A number of modern poets have used this technique, for example, T. E. Brown with his much over-rated 'A garden is a lovesome thing' and his other poems, some of which are more intelligent. However, the term 'free verse' has acquired the stricter meaning of poetry in which there is neither rhyme nor metre.

The three main kinds of free verse in modern English poetry seem to be: strict forms borrowed from other languages, with counting of syllables, patterns of line length, symmetries of cadence outside the formulae of English metre, and so on; incantatory verse with rhythms suggesting the Bible, Oriental sacred literature or other religious works; and verse with a more colloquial style, suitable for the expression of difficult thought or sometimes of cynicism or the 'man-of-the-world' attitude.[1]

Examples of the first type are 'H.D.' (Hilda Doolittle), who has tried to give something of the cool, crisp, restrained effect of Greek lyric, with patterns of vowels or consonants playing a large part in her technique; Adelaide Crapsey (*d.* 1914), a minor American poet who imitated the Japanese *hokku* in beautiful little five-line poems which she called *cinquains*; Ezra Pound in some poems that are imitations or translations of the Greek or Chinese; and Marianne Moore who practises a strict symmetry.

Incantatory free verse is to be found, in a sense, as early as Macpherson's *Ossian* and Blake's prophecies; these are un-rhymed and irregular, though the latter are rather more rhythmical than contemporary free verse. Walt Whitman and D. H. Lawrence are the most important of the moderns to have used this kind of verse. At its best it is magnificent; at its

[1] I do not use this in any condemnatory sense.

worst it slides into pseudo-prophecy that is embarrassingly bad. Edith Sitwell is one of the prophetic poets with the fewest lapses from self-criticism, probably because she has also a scholarly understanding of poetic technique.

A more colloquial kind of free verse, which at its best has a ring of great sincerity and naturalness, is to be found in such poets as Richard Aldington, Herbert Read, the bitter American poet Robinson Jeffers, in a few poems by T. S. Eliot, though he in general uses new variants on metre more than true free verse, and some of Auden and MacNeice, though their most masterly poems are probably those using rhyme or partial rhyme. The student who wants to understand something of the technique of good free verse should look at some of the work of each of the poets mentioned in this chapter and should not take on trust what certain cautious and lazy people say about it; much of pattern and discipline is to be found in it, though the internal pattern of sounds, the choice of exact words and the effect of associations gives it its beauty. The student is also warned that there is plenty of very poor free verse about just as there is plenty of very poor conventional verse, and also that the greater part of twentieth-century poetry is not written in this form.

XVII. THE CHOICE OF WORDS

Thy words are like a cloud of winged snakes.
SHELLEY: *Prometheus Unbound*

POETRY is made of words, and obviously the choice of words is important in poetry; indeed, in a sense it is the whole art of writing poetry. We have already considered the choice of words from the point of view of their accentuation (producing rhythm), their sound (producing onomatopoeic and rhyme effects) and their associative value; but a little attention ought also to be paid to the choice of words for their actual 'intellectual' meaning. This sounds so obvious as to be foolish, but inexperienced students of poetry sometimes forget all about it in the excitement of studying techniques of rhythm and pattern.

We may assume that the poet knows more or less what he wants to say before he sits down to write a poem. One does not usually sit down before a sheet of blank paper with a blank mind. An image has come into the poet's head; a rhythm is singing in the poet's ear; perhaps a logical sequence has already shaped itself and the choice of words will be dictated by these considerations. However, if we look at a manuscript left by any well-known poet we shall nearly always find that the poet has made many erasures and alterations before arriving at the final version. This process of polishing is very important. During the polishing, the poet is usually dealing with individual words; he may exclude a word because its sound echoes or clashes with the sound of another where such an effect is not wanted.

> And in his grave the weird worms squirm

would be a line of appalling badness; it would be some improvement to say:

> And in his grave the long worms creep.

The poet may find that in the excitement of composition he has wrenched an accent unnaturally or committed some inaccuracy of fact; he may become doubtful of the strict meaning of a word, or its accentuation, and need to check this in the dictionary; but most polishing is probably done in a search for the *mot juste*, the most exact and effective word possible in the context.

Unless the poet is aiming at some special sound effect of repetitive magic, he will usually try to convey his meaning in as few words as possible, a virtue which is equally applicable to good prose. The poets of the 1930s[1] who were so concise that their enemies described their work as 'telegraphese' were not merely being tiresome; aiming at crisp conciseness, they may have exceeded, but they were trying to do something entirely sensible and desirable, to concentrate as much meaning as possible into every line. The Imagists in their Manifesto, an important document in the history of poetry, said: 'Finally, most of us believe that concentration is the very essence of poetry.'[2] Almost all critical statements as general as this, like

[1] Auden, Day Lewis, Spender.

[2] The 'Imagist Anthologies' were published in 1914, 1915, 1916 and 1917; the chief contributors were Amy Lowell, D. H. Lawrence, F. S. Flint, Richard Aldington, H.D., and Ezra Pound.

most other dogmas and generalizations, are overstatements and exclude something that is worth considering, but the reader should ponder over this statement. How often is it a temptation to 'pad' a piece of written work in the hope of making it look more impressive! And there is an additional reason for wanting to 'pad' in poetry; two or three more words may be needed to fill out the line metrically. Happy is the poet who has sufficient integrity to refuse to 'pad'!

The words that can most easily be altered in polishing a poem are adjectives and adverbs. Let us first look at a few examples of brilliantly appropriate adjectives:

> The *belching* whale
> And *humming* water must o'erwhelm thy corpse,
> Lying with *simple* shells!
>> SHAKESPEARE: *Pericles*

It might be argued that water does not hum; but anyone whose head has gone under the surface of the sea during a swim will recognize the sense-impression.

> How shall your *houseless* heads and *unfed* sides,
> Your *looped* and *windowed* raggedness, defend you
> From seasons such as these?
>> SHAKESPEARE: *King Lear*

> Dancing in the *chequered* shade.
>> MILTON: *L'Allegro*

> And bid the *weltering* waves their *oozy* channel keep.
>> MILTON: *Nativity Ode*

> A *winning* wave, deserving note,
> In the *tempestuous* petticoat. . . .
>> HERRICK

> *Bubbling* runnels joined the sound;
>
> COLLINS

> Where rivulets dance their *wayward* round,
> And beauty born of *murmuring* sound
> Shall pass into her face.
>
> WORDSWORTH

> When I have fears that I may cease to be,
> Before my pen has gleaned my *teeming* brain,
> Before *high-piled* books, in charactery,
> Hold like *rich* garners the *full-ripened* grain. . . .
>
> KEATS

We have only to replace a few of these adjectives with others that do not spoil the metre, in order to appreciate the greater aptness of those the poets used:

> Dancing in the spotted shade. . . .

> A pretty wave, deserving note,
> In the tumultuous petticoat. . . .

> Streaming runnels joined the sound. . . .

In two of the above examples we have also brought in an excess of those annoying s's.

It has, however, been suggested that whereas an immature poet gains all his best effects of apt description from his adjectives, a mature great poet gains fewer effects from adjectives and more from verbs. There is an interesting example of how the importance of verbs increases in Wordsworth's *Prelude*; the 1805 version is the fresher and probably the more sincere, for the poet of the 1850 version had declined to conventionality, a disastrous quality in poets; but the style has been improved in the later version. Often Wordsworth replaced a colourless 'was' or 'is' by some more definite verb:

> 1805.   The sea was laughing at a distance. . . .
> 1850.   The sea lay laughing at a distance.

Similarly in Wordsworth's *Michael* the first version:

> Beside the brook
> There is a straggling heap of unhewn stones!

The later version is:

> Beside the brook
> Appears a straggling heap of unhewn stones!

When Pope in his translation of the *Iliad* replaces

> Destruction hovers o'er yon devoted wall

by

> Destruction hangs o'er yon devoted wall

the reason is obvious. Here are some examples of very apt verbs from well-known poems:

> Save where the beetle *wheels* his droning flight
> GRAY: *Elegy*

> Ride ten thousand daies and nights
> Till age *snow* white hairs on thee;
> DONNE

> And the caked snow is *shuffled*
> From the ploughboy's heavy shoon . . .
> KEATS

> *Shine* out, little head, *sunning* over with curls. . . .
> TENNYSON

Ah Love! could thou and I with Fate *conspire*
To *grasp* this sorry Scheme of Things entire,
Would we not *shatter* it to bits, and then
Remould it nearer to the Heart's Desire!
    FITZGERALD: *Rubaiyat of Omar Khayyam*

    Where our sheep
Half asleep
Tinkle homeward through the twilight, *stray* or
       stop
As they *crop*—

             BROWNING

How neatly 'tinkle' both suggests the sound, and, by telling
us that the sheep are wearing bells, also suggests that the scene
is exotic!

The chidden billow seems to *pelt* the clouds;
    SHAKESPEARE: *Othello*

Ram thou thy fruitful tidings in mine ears . . .
    SHAKESPEARE: *Antony and Cleopatra*

Why should I write this down, that's *riveted*,
Screw'd to my memory?
    SHAKESPEARE: *Cymbeline*

Perhaps contemporary writers are more self-consciously
concerned about the apt word than writers have ever been;
this extreme self-consciousness often leads them into slight
pedantry or what may look like misplaced cleverness; but
more often it produces something refreshingly original that
has arisen out of careful observation, alert imagination and
well-stocked vocabulary. The last quality is a necessary one
for a good poet; if he is to choose strictly accurate words, he

must know the words first, just as all of us, if we are to avoid clichés in our prose writing, must be capable of putting together our own expressive phrases. Originality is one of the perennial delights of poetry; and one of the curious facts about it is that what seems most original is also often what is most true and exact. Perhaps the pleasurable surprise we receive whenever we notice a particularly apt word is an indictment of our general lack of precision in speech and writing!

may possibly also be thinking of the scythes on the wheels of Ancient British chariots, which most horribly 'reaped the field'. The laurels planted by warriors on the field manured with blood (I think we are meant to understand line 10 in this brutal way; blood is good manure for the laurels of military fame) catch up the garlands on the brows of conquerors and are contrasted with the flowers of the actions of the just; the flowers smell sweet; blood and laurels both have an unpleasant smell.

The actions of the just are presented as some loved, unobtrusive flower such as the violet. There is a subtle use of associations in the use of garlands and laurels as a symbol for the wrong kind of fame and the use of captives led to the altar as a symbol for death. For sacrificial victims are garlanded:

> To what green altar, O mysterious priest,
> Lead'st thou that heifer lowing to the skies,
> And all her silken flanks with garlands dressed?
> KEATS: *Ode on a Grecian Urn*

There is thus a hint that in acquiring laurels the warriors are really preparing themselves for the sacrificial altar. 'Purple', too, is associated with royal and triumphal robes as well as with blood; the sound-echo in 'victor-victim' and even the brilliant use of 'blood' in the first line all help to build us a half-conscious acceptance of an actual equating of fame with death. It is a wonderful piece of virtuosity in the handling of associations and ambiguous words. We may also be meant to think of the wreaths used at funerals.

This seems at first sight a rather ordinary poem, and we wonder why it moves and haunts us until we begin to analyse these cross-currents.

XIX. HOW NOT TO
APPROACH POETRY

Polonius: This is too long.
Hamlet : It shall to the barber's, with your beard. Prithee,
say on; he's for a jig, or a tale of bawdry, or he
sleeps.

SHAKESPEARE: *Hamlet*

THE practice of setting pieces of poetry to be commented upon in an examination ought to be a good test of sensitivity, intelligence and self-expression; unfortunately, it can also be a test of mere glibness. It is easy to pick up a critical vocabulary and a few clichés of criticism. It is easy to pretend that we like something when we are not really interested; it is easy to pretend we disapprove of something we like if we think this is what is expected of us; and it is sometimes easier to write fluently about something in which we are not interested than about something we really love and revere. It is easy to count syllables and gain a few marks by being able to do arithmetic. Even more disastrously easy is the habit of using a few words like 'effective', 'beautiful' and 'expressive' and a few simple technical terms like 'figurative' and 'personification' without knowing anything worth knowing about poetry. Women students, with many generations of enforced docility behind them, are perhaps even more prone to this kind of glibness than men, though there are already plenty of good women critics.[1]

One of the most pathetic things about present-day literary education is that, except for those who go to a university to take a specialist course in English Literature, most of the people who are taught to read poetry and write about it at school never wish to read it again. There are many reasons for this; bad teaching is probably the main reason, and bad teaching is not entirely the fault of the teachers, who are themselves often people who have been badly taught or who have the kind of emotional difficulties that make it painful to approach poetry sincerely. Other reasons are: the debasing influence of most newspapers and magazines; the popularity of novels;[2] the competition of the cinema, radio and television for our leisure interests; the general appalling standard of speech in this country, which makes most people unfit to read poetry aloud even in the family circle;[3] the sheer low intelligence of many people—which is nobody's fault; the difficulty of much poetry when we no longer have notes and teachers available to explain the obsolete words or allusions; and the view, common in England, that we ought to hide our emotions, which gives us the erroneous impression that emotional poetry is somehow weak and unmanly. I think one reason is

[1] For example: Helen Gardner, Catherine Ing, Vivienne Koch, Kathleen Raine, Janet Spens, Edith Sitwell, Virginia Woolf.

[2] I do not, of course, mean that novels are not worth reading.

[3] A warning may be offered here. Anyone who wants to acquire a higher standard of speech is in danger of falling a prey to some charlatan who will teach affected speech and do more harm than good. Coaching in speech should be sought from someone who has the Diploma of the Speech Fellowship or the L.R.A.M. (Eloc.)., or some other recognised qualifications.

that too many of us learn to be glib and to say approximately the right things in order to earn marks or praise, a weakness which may continue into our whole social life. The whole business becomes a habit of cant and hypocrisy.[1]

I cannot suggest how this can be entirely avoided; if we are to have the criticism of poetry on examination papers, some degree of 'cramming' is sure to happen; if we leave poetry out of 'set books' and off examination papers, poetry will probably be read less rather than more; and the study of a subject for an examination does not automatically spoil it for us. Yet it may be helpful to say something about the two main kinds of false criticism that most people not professional critics are likely to perpetrate.[2]

The first kind is *Pleasing the Examiners*, or pleasing schoolmasters, schoolmistresses, lecturers, tutors, professors or anyone else who is temporarily in authority over us. We all have to set ourselves to please Authority at some time in our lives in order to enjoy some measure of success and financial security; but the best attitude to pleasing Authority is one of cheerful utilitarian cynicism. Similarly, a certain cheerful cynicism is sometimes the best attitude to examinations, tests which are necessary but really prove very little. The examination attitude to a poem sometimes has to be: 'What can I say about this? What will sound most learned and impressive?' The sincere private attitude is more like this: 'I like this—it does something to me. I wonder why. I will pull it to pieces and see. How interesting! So that is how he makes me feel as if the top of my head had been removed! Now it seems even better.'

[1] See Thorstein Veblen: *Theory of the Leisure Class*.

[2] Professional critics also make plenty of mistakes, but their falsities can be made only with a good deal of knowledge such as the reader of this book has not.

Or, since in the course of a life in which much poetry is read we are bound to meet some that is inferior, we may react thus: 'I don't think much of that; I wonder why not; it strikes me as a sham. Let me have another look at it.' And then, either, 'I see, yes, my first instinct was right, because . . .', or perhaps, 'Goodness, I'd missed the point completely; I was reading it the wrong way.'[1]

To an alert-minded lover of poetry a poem is not spoiled by being analysed; it becomes richer and more fascinating. The wrong way to approach a poem is to analyse it when you do not really want to. Yes, I know you often have to do this in an examination; nobody but a person with natural literary talent can be completely sincere about a poem in a room full of desks, with a clock to look at and other questions to answer and in the presence of an examiner who is well supplied with more paper, red pencil, string, sealing-wax, lists of candidates and a bottle of sal volatile. The only genuine criticism likely to appear in an examination is on something that has been prepared beforehand. You will gain nothing, neither pleasure nor profit, by reading poetry because you think you ought to. If you want to enjoy poetry, it is probably best to stray about among books, to ask people to read it to you, to listen to broadcast poetry and generally to relax and let poetry happen to you. If you can develop a sincere liking for poetry, you will soon develop alert critical intelligence about it.

From examination criticism you will at least learn something about the technical side of poetry, which is worth knowing, just as by dissecting a rabbit you will learn something about anatomy though you may not develop love of animals. It is perhaps unfortunate that the age at which we

[1] Strictly, 'bad poetry' is a contradiction in terms; all 'poetry' that is bad should be called merely 'verse' to distinguish it from prose.

take important formal examinations is generally that during which our emotional and aesthetic susceptibilities are developing, or should be. Examinations help some people to develop, especially if the teachers are good; but they often hinder other people. However, it is never too late to develop the capacity to enjoy poetry or any other art. The now-famous American painter known as 'Grandma Moses' began painting at the age of seventy. My father, about six weeks before he died at the age of fifty-seven, suddenly had a new burst of aesthetic experience and 'discovered' contemporary poetry with immense enthusiasm and intelligence, after sneering at it for years.

The second kind of false criticism may be called the attitude of *Be Nothing if not Critical*. This is caused in part by the fact that the word *criticism*, which in literary contexts means the assessment of literature, in everyday contexts means only finding fault. Some teachers, trying to counter the fault-finding associations of the word *criticism*, make the association even stronger by speaking of *criticism and appreciation*. The really able critic is as often someone who can show us good where we did not see it before, as the fault-finder, and is a much pleasanter person.

Another reason for excessive fault-finding in criticism is the desire to sound clever and different. This is not surprising in young students. The idolatry lavished on Shakespeare by some school teachers is enough to make any healthy youngster revolt, especially as the idolatry is all too often insincere. We also tend to turn against what we liked in childhood and early adolescence, to prove to ourselves that we have put behind us these periods in which we were unimportant, misunderstood and miserable. We should bear in mind that every strong enthusiasm may turn to dislike in a later reaction, and we should always make allowances for this possibility. We are bound to rebel not only against our own early judgments, but against the judgments of the previous generation; our parents' generation is the one that has imposed Authority upon us by force, and if we do not rise up against it and throw off our mental restrictions we shall never progress to the maturity which will enable us to see another generation's point of view. Mankind progresses thus:

> Drive your cart and your plough over the bones of the dead.
>
> BLAKE

However, once we have liberated ourselves by this whole-some and necessary rebellion, we should feel free also to look round and pick up all the things we threw away that are now worth keeping; selection is a much more mature response to anything than indiscriminate rejection.

We should not go on sneering and destroying one day longer than we need; during our emancipation period we are not pleasant to live with, and we are often thinking of the effect of what we are saying, rather than its truth. When I was about seventeen my father was very fond of using Milton as a stick with which to beat the moderns whom I had already learned to love; I am very glad to say that I vividly remember shouting abuse of Milton at my father, weeping with fury. I am certain that I was right to go my own way; we learn far more by insisting on our freedom than by sitting meekly at someone's feet; the brutal and painful break has to be made. But I do not delude myself that I was lovable at the time; once I was free, I learned to love Milton also, and to go on abusing him when I had escaped from Authority would have been merely silly and weak. Some people never get beyond this first stage of healthy rebellion.

The quickest way to break oneself of a habit of sneering or destructive criticism is to try to write poetry. I should like to hear of millions of English people trying to write poetry. It does not matter if it is bad; it is not likely to be published; there is room in literature as in sport for the 'rabbit', the amateur[1] who plays only for the fun of the thing. To write even the poorest verses is to learn something about the skill needed to write good ones.

However, the principal cause of destructive and unfair criticism is sheer ignorance. Many stupid things are said about Shakespeare and Chaucer, Donne and Tennyson, because they were writing in different eras and wrote taking for granted certain values and supposed facts which are now exploded. We should always try to see a poem in its historical setting, especially if we do not like it at first sight. It is foolish to expect every writer of every period to take for granted the same values as ourselves; in another hundred or even twenty years the accepted values will have undergone another change and our own writers will need to be seen in their historical setting to be fully appreciated. Though it is possible to enjoy a great deal of poetry without understanding either the history of poetry or the rudiments of national history, these studies help us a great deal by enriching our appreciation of allusions and emotions no longer current.

Ignorance cannot, however, do much harm to the reputations of the long-established great dead. Where it does most harm is in the assessment of the work of the living. The work of the living poet is almost heartbreaking. It is difficult to get a volume of poetry published, because so little is bought that the publisher loses on it, and unless he is a prosperous pub-

[1] 'Amateur' means 'lover'; we are generally much wiser over what we love than over what we hate.

lisher he cannot take the risk. The poet is lonely, because he has the task of being sincere in a community in which the cinema, the popular Press and all too many schools do their best to dilute, cheapen or repress emotion. The five poets of repute who are my personal friends and the fifty or so others with whom I have at some time had correspondence have all been pleasant, friendly, natural people, with none of the affectations the cartoonists and cheap novelists give to their unreal 'literary men', but poets, however lovable personally, have a great loneliness to face. Their worst enemies are the timid people with false culture who spend their time sneering at everything that is fresh, sincere, new and interesting. The great dead poets should have the sympathy and love of the young; the lonely living poets need it. It is to the young whose minds are not yet frozen into poses that the living poets turn for their audience. If every student in a university or training college and every person under thirty-five bought—as a sacrifice to British culture—one new book of poetry every year, we might see a cultural development in this country that would be as dramatic as the flowering of English poetry in the great Elizabethan age. To every student who has learned a little from this book, that is my last word.

SOME BOOKS FOR
FURTHER READING

Anthologies of English Poetry, for 'dipping'

RICHARD ALDINGTON: *Poetry of the English-Speaking World.* This is the finest single-volume collection of English poetry I have seen; it is the most representative, and the poems are arranged in a roughly chronological order that is useful for enabling the reader to see the general perspective.

F. T. PALGRAVE: *The Golden Treasury of Songs and Lyrics.* Various cheap editions are available, e.g. in the World's Classics and Everyman series. It is still a most useful anthology.

The Oxford Book of Ballads.
The Oxford Book of Carols.
The Oxford Book of Sixteenth Century Verse.
The Oxford Book of Seventeenth Century Verse.
The Oxford Book of Eighteenth Century Verse.
The Oxford Book of Regency Verse.
The Oxford Book of Victorian Verse.
The Oxford Book of Modern Verse.

All these collections are scholarly, wide in scope, cheap in proportion to their content and so beautifully printed and bound that it is a joy to handle them. *The Oxford Book of English Verse*, equally beautiful to look at, is

rather pedestrian as compared with the others and seems
to me to be superseded by Aldington's anthology.

OSCAR WILLIAMS: *A Little Treasury of Modern Poetry.*

The widest in scope of the anthologies of contemporary
British and American poetry; very well indexed.

ANNE RIDLER: *A Little Book of Modern Verse.*

MICHAEL ROBERTS: *The Faber Book of Modern Verse.*

GEOFFREY GRIGSON: *Poetry of the Present.*

Useful in that it represents many good minor poets who
are not otherwise well known.

Some Books of Stimulating Criticism

(The reader is warned not to read criticism before having read
plenty of assorted poetry!)

ROBERT GRAVES: *On English Poetry.*

The Common Asphodel.

Not everyone will support all the theories of Mr. Graves,
but all he has to say is worth pondering and most admir-
ably expressed.

E. M. W. TILLYARD: *Poetry Direct and Oblique.*

A very small book which is, to my mind, a 'must'.

C. DAY LEWIS: *Poetry for You.*

A book intended for children but helpful to all inexperienced readers.

The Poetic Image.

More advanced.

HENRY TREECE: *How I See Apocalypse.*

A sincere book, much better than its title suggests.

FRANCIS SCARFE: *Auden and After.*

Not great criticism, but a useful guide-book to the
present age.

I. A. RICHARDS: *Practical Criticism.*

> The title might be misleading. This book is a fascinating and alarming account of what happened when Mr. Richards submitted a number of poems, without the name of the author, to a group of students. It is disturbing to all teachers and consoling to the student who has made a blunder.

Principles of Literary Criticism.

> An advanced book, well worth reading when the student is ready for it.

WILLIAM EMPSON: *Some Versions of Pastoral.*

Seven Types of Ambiguity.

The Structure of Complex Words.

> Three brilliant and exciting works of criticism; but they are all very advanced indeed and should not be tackled until the student is ready for them. *Seven Types of Ambiguity* is perhaps the easiest.

CHARLES WILLIAMS: *The English Poetic Mind.*

Poetry at Present.

> Two very exciting books, beautifully written, quite easy to read and highly provocative.

T. R. HENN: *The Apple and the Spectroscope.*

> A good book for those whose original bent is scientific.

HERBERT READ: *Collected Essays in Literary Criticism.*

> Rather advanced, but contains some very thought-provoking essays in the first half of the book.

Criticism of Historical Interest.

G. PUTTENHAM: *The Art of English Poesie.*

> An interesting example of the early approach to poetry, founded on the classics, but written with much learning and some humour by a genial critic. This book is not likely to be available except in large libraries, as it is

obtainable by itself only in an expensive edition; but it is to be found in G. Gregory Smith: *Elizabethan Critical Essays*.

SIR PHILIP SIDNEY: *Apologie for Poetrie*.
Frequently reprinted. A classic.

SAMUEL JOHNSON: *Lives of the English Poets*.
Preface to Shakespeare.
Eminently readable studies by the greatest eighteenth-century critic; some of his views nowadays seem wrong-headed, but he always has at least blunt common sense and a manly style.

SHELLEY: *A Defence of Poetry*.
The romantic attitude undiluted; lovely prose.

WORDSWORTH: *The Prelude*.
Subtitled, 'The Growth of a Poet's Mind', this is a great autobiography and most illuminating concerning not only Wordsworth, but the poetic mind in general. The 1805 version, published by Oxford University Press, is probably to be preferred.

DRYDEN: *MacFlecknoe*.

POPE: *Essay on Criticism*.
The Dunciad.

BYRON: *English Bards and Scotch Reviewers*.

ROY CAMPBELL: *The Georgiad*.
When we read satire, we probably feel sad that poets can be so cruel to each other; but we laugh. . . .

Four Stimulating Books for those who have to teach Poetry

JOHN F. DANBY: *Approach to Poetry*.

MARJORIE HOURD: *The Education of the Poetic Spirit*.

T. W. SUSSAMS: *Poetry and the Teacher*.

P. GURREY: *The Appreciation of Poetry*.

INDEX

Index

Index

184

Index

185

Index

187

Index